On the Road: Saving/Paying for College

Sheryl Garrett, CFP®
Series Editor

Adapted and compiled by
Ellen Schneid Coleman

Dearborn™
Trade Publishing
A **Kaplan Professional** Company

President, Dearborn Publishing: Roy Lipner
Vice President and Publisher: Cynthia A. Zigmund
Senior Acquisitions Editor: Mary B. Good
Cover Design: Design Solutions

© 2006 by Dearborn Financial Publishing, Inc.

Published by Dearborn Trade Publishing
A Kaplan Professional Company

A Stonesong Press Book

Project Manager: Ellen Schneid Coleman
Interior Design: Brad Walrod/High Text Graphics, Inc.

Printed in the United States of America

06 07 08   10 9 8 7 6 5 4 3 2 1

Library of Congress Cataloging-in-Publication Data
Saving/paying for college/edited by Sheryl Garrett; adapted and compiled by Ellen Schneid Coleman.
    p.   cm.—(On the road)
  Includes index.
  ISBN 1-4195-0045-7 (5 × 7.375 pbk.)
    1. College costs—United States.   2. Education—United States—Finance.
3. Scholarships—United States.   4. Student aid—United States.   I. Garrett,
Sheryl.   II. Coleman, Ellen Schneid.   III. On the road (Chicago, Ill.)
LB2342.S335 2005
379.3′8—dc22   2005015090

Dearborn Trade books are available at special quantity discounts to use for sales promotions, employee premiums, or educational purposes. Please call our Special Sales Department to order or for more information at 800-621-9621, ext. 4444, e-mail trade@dearborn.com, or write to Dearborn Trade Publishing, 30 South Wacker Drive, Suite 2500, Chicago, IL 60606-7481.

Contents

Introduction

On the Road: Saving/Paying for College is part of a new series of books from Dearborn Trade Publishing intended to help you deal with the financial issues, problems, and decisions concerning specific life events. The things to consider and the decisions you face when you're planning your child's education are obviously very different from the decision to buy a car, or even a house, for example. In fact, except perhaps for funding your retirement, they are very different from just about any other financial planning decision you might make.

Funding your child's education might be one of the most rewarding adventures you can take. After all, what is more exciting than seeing your children grow, thrive, and expand their horizon? What is more rewarding than knowing you are helping your child set off well-prepared on life's adventures? After all, a college (and perhaps graduate or professional education) not only allows your child to earn more in a lifetime, but it also provides career choices and lifestyle options.

It's a big undertaking, and in the best of all worlds you will have plenty of time to plan it. When is the best time to begin? Many parents today begin thinking of college for their kids as soon as they are born. If you are one of those parents, congratulations! But even if you are further down the road, and your child is in middle or high school, you still have a lot of options. Because financial planning shouldn't be intimidating, we created these books to take away the terror. *On the Road* books are like travel guides, which will help you make the best financial decisions at each stage of your life; in this case, when you are ready to begin investing and saving or looking for alternate sources of financing your child's education. There's another benefit of reading this book—and it's not a small one—if you've never invested in stocks, bonds, and/or mutual funds, you'll get quick insights as to what it's all about.

Now, let's take a look at where we're going. This book addresses questions that concern you *now* as you embark on the journey of saving for your child's education. Before you take the first step, try to find the answers to the following questions:

1. How does funding your child's education fit in with your other financial goals, like buying a home or funding retirement?
2. How much can you afford to save and invest toward building an education fund?
3. How much will college cost when your kid turns 18?
4. What type of account(s) should you put your money in?
5. Where should you put this money—stocks, bonds, or mutual funds?
6. Could you benefit by working with a financial advisor?
7. Where else can you and/or your child find money to pay for college?

These financial decisions are a crucial part of your family's journey, so we've made them easy to navigate, with lots of helpful "Roadmaps" (charts and tables of financial information to help you with each issue or decision that comes up) and "Tollbooths" that help you calculate your expenses or savings. We have also included "Hazard" signs that caution you on money pitfalls to watch out for. We've made sure you'll know what we're talking about, by providing "Learn the Language" definitions of unfamiliar or technical terms particular to each financial topic. And we've included "Postcards" that tell helpful stories of how other people have made successful financial journeys.

Finally, we've included an "Itinerary," a recap about all the important steps you should take—all of which are covered in detail in the six chapters of this book. You can use this as a reminder at each stage of your journey toward providing for your child's educational needs. The end of the book also includes a list of other resources to turn to if you want more in-depth information on the topics we will discuss.

We hope you find this "travel" guide helpful as you map your route to financial success and peace of mind. Life is an adventure, and money paves the way. So let's get started on the road: The light is green, put your pedal to the metal, and go!

Hiking the "College Trail"
Defining Your Financial Goals

For most people, education is an important part of life. A good education always pays! As the world continues to grow more competitive and technologically sophisticated, most of the high-paying jobs will require skills learned in college and graduate school. Years ago, most employers expected workers to have at least a high school diploma; today, a college degree is considered a minimum requirement for most well-paying jobs.

What's more, numerous studies have shown that the gap between earnings of college and high school graduates widens every year. In 1975, the average college graduate made 57 percent more than the average high school grad. By 2000, the difference had widened—the average college graduate's income was 91 percent more than that of the high school graduates (after adjusting for inflation). According to the U.S. Census Bureau, the average income in 2000 for someone with a bachelor's degree was $51,700, while someone with only a high school diploma earned an average of just $27,100. That's just about half the income of the college graduate!

Over a working lifetime, the College Board estimates that a typical college graduate earns about 75 percent more than a high school graduate does (on average, over $1 million more), and if you add a graduate degree the difference is even greater (as much as $2 million more). It's no wonder that most parents want to do all they can to help provide at least a college education for their children!

For most of us, saving for college is not our only goal—or necessity—for that matter. But before you can decide *how* and *how much* to save for college, you first need to decide *whether* you want to save for college. In other words, it is important to set your financial goals and to investigate all your options. If you have decided to save for your child's education, it is important to understand that goal in context with your other goals. This will help you create a sensible plan that will get you there. In both cases, understanding your goals will help you gain control over your finances and set you on the right path. What's more, having a goal motivates you to follow a money-management plan.

► Choosing Your Destination: Saving for College vs. Saving for Other Things

To begin with, it is important to define your goals in specific attainable terms (such as "I will save enough money for Joe's college education, which will begin in 12 years").

Set specific financial objectives and put them in writing—list dollar amounts and note exactly when you will need the money. It will motivate you to achieve your goals. Most people never set goals because they have convinced themselves that they will never reach their targets. This is unfortunate because it is a proven fact that if you don't define your goals, you won't accomplish them. In this chapter you will find several easy-to-fill-out

Hazard!

Synchronize Your Goals

If you are a couple, consider making copies of Roadmaps 1.1 through 1.3 and *separately* completing your own list of prioritized goals. After you've completed your individual lists, meet to discuss what you have in common and any differences you may have. Together, create a third list that represents your combined goals and priorities. With this level of careful thought and discussion, you can move on to the next leg of this trip with a solid, agreed-upon plan.

Dear Jan,

You know I was never good about saving; when we were kids my allowance was gone the day I got it. And, even though I make a great income as a loan officer—of all things!—I never put money aside. You won't believe it, but it's true, once I started tracking my spending after Dan left and learned how to work out a budget, it made a "million percent" difference in my life.

I've created a savings account and am putting away money to buy a house, and I'm even more motivated to save for Susan's college education. I know she's only two, but it's never too early to start. Sis, you and Steve should think about doing this for Timmy, too. After all, he's going on five and college is just around the corner!

Love,
Debbie

worksheets that will help you determine your highest financial priorities and how you can achieve them.

You can't reach all of your goals overnight—and funding a college education is a significant goal—but knowing what they are, and which ones are most important to you, will help you fulfill them faster. Because setting goals is really another way of defining priorities, the process helps you use your limited resources and income effectively to attain your highest priorities. By crystallizing your aspirations, you can take charge of your life and control your money for the purposes you find most important.

Don't think that goal setting is too hard; you've been doing it for most of your life. When you last started a diet, you set a specific goal for how many pounds you would trim. When you were on the track team in high school, you set a goal to achieve a particular time for your event—a four-minute mile, for instance. As you went through college, you set your sights on a certain grade-point average or you worked really hard to get into the graduate school of your choice. All you are doing now is applying that same discipline to your personal finances.

Many of you share finances with a spouse or partner; therefore, goal setting must be done mutually. To avoid friction, you must agree, for the most part, with your spouse or significant other on which goals get the highest priority. The first thing you need to do is decide on the goals mutually—that way you can avoid financial arguments.

Also, remember that as you accomplish certain goals during your life, you must constantly be setting new ones. For example, once your children's college educations have been paid for, you might want to shift priorities in order to set aside money for a second home or travel or add more money to your retirement savings.

▶ Before Loading Your Knapsack: Get a Handle on Your Goals

There are three kinds of goals: short, medium, and long-term. Within each of these three categories, you not only have goals but also priorities for those goals. Like most of us, you will probably never have enough money to achieve all your goals over the next year; therefore, you have to allocate some resources on an ongoing basis to each of the three categories so that you have some chance of accomplishing them over time. Many people neglect the medium- and long-term goals in favor of the seemingly more pressing short-term goals, but that only puts off the day of reckoning. The longer you delay starting to accumulate the money for longer-term goals like buying a home or funding college education for your children or retirement, the more difficult the realization of those goals becomes.

It would be hard to find two people with absolutely identical goals. Your goals depend on your interests, values, and your lifestyle. In this chapter you will find worksheets that will help you formulate your goals in each of the three categories. After you locate one of your goals on the worksheet, note the amount of money you will need to achieve it, how high a priority it has compared to your other goals, and when you would like to achieve it. Okay —it's time to set off.

Mini Vacations: Short-Term Goals. Short-term goals are those you would like to achieve within the next year (see Roadmap 1.1). These might include paying off your credit cards, buying certain large items like a car, or furniture, or taking a much-needed vacation. If you don't know the exact cost of any of the items on your list, estimate it for now.

Roadmap 1.1

Short-Term Goals Worksheet

Goal	Priority	Date to Accomplish	$ Amount Needed
Build up Emergency Reserve (minimum three months' salary)	_____	_____	_____
Draft Wills and Health Care Directives	_____	_____	_____
Buy Adequate Insurance	_____	_____	_____
Auto	_____	_____	_____
Health	_____	_____	_____
Home	_____	_____	_____
Life	_____	_____	_____
Contribute to Charity Name _____	_____	_____	_____
Fund IRA or Keogh Account	_____	_____	_____
Increase Contribution to Company Benefit Plan	_____	_____	_____
Join a Health/Sports Club	_____	_____	_____
Make Major Home Improvements	_____	_____	_____
Make Major Purchases	_____	_____	_____
Pay Off Bills	_____	_____	_____
Pay Off Credit Cards	_____	_____	_____
Save for Holiday Gifts, Birthdays, etc.	_____	_____	_____
Take Vacation	_____	_____	_____
Other (specify) _____	_____	_____	_____
TOTAL $ AMOUNT NEEDED			$ _____

Two-Week Holiday: Medium-Term Goals. Medium-term goals are those for which it takes between two and 10 years to accumulate the money (see Roadmap 1.2). These may include building a down payment for a first or second home, creating a college fund for children older than eight, or saving to take the overseas trip of your dreams.

Round-the-World Cruise: Long-Term Goals. Long-term goals take more than 10 years to fulfill (see Roadmap 1.3). The most common long-term goal is a financially secure retirement, which takes a lifetime of financial discipline. Other long-term goals include paying for extensive travel, starting your own business, going back to school to receive a higher degree of education, buying a vacation home, and making sure you can afford medical attention in your later years.

What Else Is Going in Your Knapsack? Set Priorities

Before making a major decision like deciding to save for your child's education, you must first ask yourself, "What are my financial objectives?" Let's say, for example, you're a young couple, and you both want to retire at age 65. But between now and retirement you have a long list of things you want to do—you want to send your children to private high schools, fund your children's college education, and take an annual family trip to Europe.

Before you commit to those goals, ask yourselves, "Would my goals change if I knew I had only two years left to live?" Let's say that you would not change your goals, but your spouse would like to spend less time at work and more time with the family. If that were to happen, your resources would deplete and you might not fund everything you want to do. You would then have to reconsider your goals within the context of your new circumstances and desires. Identifying your goals is not enough; you must prioritize them.

With that in mind, take a look at the goals and priorities you set in the first three roadmaps. If you are doing this with your spouse or partner, compare your priorities. Now transfer your goals (or your agreed upon combined goals) to Roadmap 1.4, the "Identified Goals Worksheet."

Even though you purchased this book because your goal is saving for college for your kids, and we assume it still is, it's essential to know what your other goals are and how saving and investing for college fits in with those plans. Starting with the goals you identified on the previous three roadmaps, enter them in the "Goals" column on Roadmap 1.4 (others may occur to you as you complete the worksheet; add them, too), then fill in the remainder

Roadmap 1.2

Medium-Term Goals Worksheet

Goal	Priority	Date to Accomplish	$ Amount Needed
Create College Fund for Children			
Child 1 _____	_____	_____	_____
Child 2 _____	_____	_____	_____
Save Down Payment for Home	_____	_____	_____
Finance Major Home Renovation	_____	_____	_____
Finance Special Occasions (weddings, bar mitzvahs, etc.)	_____	_____	_____
Help Child Finance Home	_____	_____	_____
Pay Off Education Debt	_____	_____	_____
Save for Next Child	_____	_____	_____
Take Overseas Trip	_____	_____	_____
Take Time off to Pursue an Interest	_____	_____	_____
Other (specify)			
_____	_____	_____	_____
TOTAL $ NEEDED			$_____

of the worksheet. Give each goal a number indicating its priority; that is, which goal do you want to achieve first, second, and so on. In the process, you may also discover that some of the things you thought you wanted or needed really aren't all that important compared to such things as planning your retirement or saving for college.

Roadmap 1.3

Long-Term Goals Worksheet

Goal	Priority	Date to Accomplish	$ Amount Needed
Buy Retirement Home	_____	_____	_____
Buy Vacation Home	_____	_____	_____
Continue Education	_____	_____	_____
Establish Long-Term Health Care for Self and/or Spouse	_____	_____	_____
Establish Retirement Fund	_____	_____	_____
Help Older Parents	_____	_____	_____
Make a Charitable Gift or Bequest	_____	_____	_____
Pay Off Mortgage Early	_____	_____	_____
Start a Business	_____	_____	_____
Start a New Career	_____	_____	_____
Travel Extensively	_____	_____	_____
Other (specify)	_____	_____	_____
_____			
TOTAL $ NEEDED			$ _____

As you work through the roadmap, think about which goals are really important to you and which can wait a few months or several years. What is your target date? Is it six months, one year, or six years? Every goal should have a beginning and an ending date. Once you have committed yourself to a timeframe in your mind and on paper, you have taken one more positive step toward reaching your goal.

In the earlier worksheets, you estimated those costs you weren't certain of; now is the time to get serious and more specific about this. Even if you can't know for sure what something like a college education will cost when you need it, finding out as much as possible will help you plan more realistically. By calling, reading, or shopping to determine the estimated cost of, for example, putting in a pool or paying for a college education, your goal becomes more than just a dream. (We'll talk more about how to estimate costs for college in the next chapter.)

If you have money in savings, how much of that "Amount Already Saved" do you want to use toward a particular goal? Write it down. Commit yourself to an amount (if you don't know how much you have saved, complete this portion after you have completed Roadmap 2.1 in Chapter 2).

Make sure you fill in the "How to Achieve" column on Roadmap 1.4; it is a crucial to your success in achieving your goals. What are you willing to do to make your goal a reality? Will it involve working overtime or finding a second job? Will it mean tradeoffs—cutting back or eliminating expenses such as movies, meals out, or a new car every three years—so you can reach your goal? How much will you have to save each week, month, or year to reach your goals? If you have a difficult time setting aside money for your goals, arrange with your bank for direct deposit from your paycheck.

Mountain Lake or Summer at the Shore: Kid's College or Your Retirement?

In May 2004, Opinion Research Corporation conducted a survey of college-bound teens and parents of college-bound teens on behalf of Fidelity Investments. The survey found that under ideal circumstances 93 percent of parents would be willing to help pay for their children's college education, with half willing to pay for all or most of the costs.

In our opinion, as important as it is to save for college, your first priority should be saving for your own retirement. In fact, we believe you should save at least 10 percent of your gross income for retirement—assuming you start very early. Then put another 1 percent toward college costs. For example, if your family's annual income is $50,000, try to save $5,000 per year for retirement and $500 a year for college. That breaks down to almost $100 a week for retirement and $10 a week for college. One of the best ways to do this is by setting up automatic savings plans so you never have a chance to spend this money.

Roadmap 1.4

Goals Worksheet–Immediate/Short-range Goals

Priority	Goal	Target Date	Cost Estimate	Amount Already Saved	How to Achieve (Amount per month, second job, etc.)

Goals Worksheet—Middle- and Long-range Goals

Priority	Goal	Target Date	Cost Estimate	Amount Already Saved	How to Achieve (Amount per month, second job, etc.)

Hazard!

Remember: Don't neglect your own retirement savings in favor of saving for college. There are plenty of funding sources available to help pay for college if your own savings fall short, but you're on your own for retirement.

There are many advantages to retirement savings that should not be overlooked when you are also thinking about funding your children's schooling. One of them is saving on taxes. To meet retirement goals, it is important to start saving early and utilize tax deferred, employer-provided programs, such as 401(k) and 403(b) plans, if available. In addition to allowing you to save on a pretax basis—equivalent to getting a tax deduction—these plans provide the benefit of tax-deferred compounding of the earnings within these accounts. Employer plans also provide a convenient and disciplined means to invest on a regular basis and to benefit from dollar cost averaging through up and down markets. (Dollar cost averaging means you avoid being a victim of the market. Because you always buy, say $100 worth of a certain stock a month, some months $100 buys more stock, some months less. Over time, you'll pay a median amount for each share, and not get caught buying at high prices.) Because of the "use it or lose it" nature of these accounts, as well as IRAs and Roth IRAs, maximizing annual contributions makes sense.

And saving for retirement vs. saving for a college education is not necessarily an either/or proposition. Sometimes you can have your mountain air *and* your salt water taffy. In some cases, retirement accounts can be used for both retirement and college. For example, withdrawals from Roth IRAs can be made without penalty for qualifying educational expenses, and loans can be taken from 401(k) accounts. For couples having children later in life, the need for college money may even coincide with the start of retirement, which means funds can be withdrawn from retirement accounts without penalty.

There also are tax-efficient savings programs specifically for college, like Coverdell ESA and Section 529 Plans (see Chapter 5). Another compelling reason to emphasize qualified retirement accounts is that they are usually excluded from financial aid formulas. In contrast, money held in regular taxable accounts does count in financial aid formulas. Even the Coverdell ESA and Section 529 accounts work against receiving need-based financial aid.

▶ The Road to College Is Paved with Options: Investigate Alternative Routes

Now that you've completed the four Roadmaps, let's assume that at least one of your medium- to long-term goals still is to save for your child's education. Does this mean providing every dime to get through college and perhaps graduate school, or just supporting them by cosigning student loans, matching income dollar-for-dollar, or some other way of helping out? Is it just helping out with tuition and books, or do you want to cover room and board and basic living expenses (more about these alternate routes in Chapter 6)? It is important to be clear about what this goal means to you in

Robin,

I almost feel a sense of guilt saying it, but in some ways I feel that we did too much for our kids. We had it hammered into our heads that we had to provide all the money for their college expenses,  *which we did for three kids. Two of those kids are now making more money than we will ever see. We are getting to an age where we would like to slow down and do some things for ourselves, but we won't have enough money for many years.*

I'm happy we were able to help our children as much as we did, but it seems somewhat inequitable that they have it so good and we are so far from reaching our own dream. I see now that there were other ways we could have helped them through school, and even if they had gotten loans, they could have paid them off with little stress.

I am telling you this now, because I know you are agonizing over how as a single parent you are going to send Gabriel to school, and I want you to know you have options.

Love,
Debbie

personal and financial terms because you need to assess the impact on your financial resources.

▶ Check Your Money Belt: Know Where Your Money Goes

If you have a strong desire to reach your goal and you really want your money to work for you, you must pay attention to what you do with it. To achieve long-range goals, such as college or early retirement where large amounts are necessary, these two factors are critical to your success.

How Far Have You Traveled? Tracking Your Goals

Roadmap 1.5 offers a quick worksheet that lets you track the progress you are making toward achieving your high-priority goals (make as many copies as you need; you should have one for each of these goals).

Monthly Savings Needed to Reach Goal. Let's say that you determine you need to save $100 at the beginning of every month for 10 years to reach your goal. What should you be doing with that money? You could stash it under your favorite mattress and have $12,000 at the end of 10 years. Obviously, that method is not the wisest or safest.

If you had chosen to take that monthly $100 to your bank and let it sit safely in a savings account drawing 3 to 5 percent compounded daily interest, after 10 years you would have made between $2,000 and $3,500 "free" for doing nothing more than driving to your local bank. In the meantime, you would have accumulated over $15,000 toward your goal.

On the other hand, if you were able to find an account that pays 10 percent compounded daily interest for that same $100 every month for 10 years, your reward would be an extra $4,995.61 over the 5 percent interest or an extra $8,532.42 over the mattress investment, giving you $20,532.42 toward your goal! (These figures do not take into account the inflation factor. However, the more years you have to invest and the higher interest rate or return amount you get, the more money you will accumulate.)

To figure out the monthly amount you need to invest to reach your goals, use the table in Tollbooth 1.1. The left column shows the number of years you have until you need the money for your goal. The next three columns show the divisors for three different rates of return that you can assume it is possible to earn, on average, over a long period of time. These rates of return

Roadmap 1.5

Goal-Tracking Worksheet

Goal (identify)	_____
Date in the Future You Will Need the Money	_____
How Many Years until You Need the Money	_____
Amount of Money Needed to Accomplish this Goal	_____
Money Already Accumulated for This Goal	_____
Rate of Return (%) Assumed for Accumulated Money	_____
Money Remaining to Be Accumulated for this Goal	_____
Money Needed to Be Saved Each Year at Assumed Rate of Return	_____
Monthly Amount to Be Saved (previous line divided by 12)	_____

assume you have adjusted for the effects of inflation and taxes, so they are known as real after-tax yields. The higher the rate of return, the more risk you have to take in your investment choices to achieve it (more about risk in Chapter 3).

To use the table, take the amount of money you will need to achieve your goal and pick an assumed rate of return. Then find the divisor for the number of years you have allocated to reach the goal. Simply divide your dollar goal by the divisor, and you have figured out the monthly amount of savings you need to reach your goal. The divisor automatically calculates the effect of compounding of interest, which becomes quite a powerful force over time.

For example, say you want to accumulate a $100,000 nest egg toward your child's education in 15 years. You assume a real after-tax yield of 6 percent. When you look down the 6 percent column to the 15-year line, you see the

Tollbooth 1.1

Determining the Monthly Savings Needed to Reach a Goal

	Divisors (By Real After-Tax Rates of Return)		
Years to Goal	2%	4%	6%
1	12.1	12.2	12.3
2	24.5	24.9	25.4
3	37.1	38.2	39.3
4	49.9	51.9	54.1
5	63.1	66.2	69.8
6	76.5	81.1	86.4
7	90.2	96.6	104.1
8	104.2	112.7	122.8
9	118.4	129.5	142.7
10	133.0	146.9	163.9
11	147.8	165.1	186.3
12	163.0	184.0	210.1
13	178.5	203.6	235.4
14	194.2	224.0	262.3
15	210.4	245.3	290.8
16	226.8	267.4	321.1
17	243.6	290.4	353.2
18	260.7	314.3	387.3
19	278.2	339.2	423.6
20	296.1	365.1	462.0
21	314.2	392.1	502.9
22	332.8	420.1	546.2
23	351.8	449.3	592.2
24	371.2	479.6	641.1
25	390.9	511.2	693.0

divisor of 290.8. Divide $100,000 by 290.8. You have to save $343.88 a month to meet your goal.

Here's another example for a shorter-term goal: Say you need $2,000 in two years to buy furniture for your living room. Assuming a 2 percent rate of return, you divide $2,000 by the divisor of 24.5 to come up with a monthly savings target of $81.63.

In Chapters 3 and 4, we'll explore how your can effectively invest your hard-earned money to reach your goals.

How Will You Pay for this Trip? Checking Your Cash Flow

With your short-, medium-, and long-term goals clearly defined, you should be feeling better already. And the fun is just beginning. Now that you know what your financial goals are, it's time to do a detailed analysis of where your money is coming from and where it is being spent. In the world of financial planning it is known as a cash flow analysis because it allows you to trace your sources and uses of money.

Even though it is a simple exercise, most people never get around to it. At the end of each month they are left wondering "Where did all my money go?" and they anxiously wait for their next paycheck so they can pay their bills. By doing the cash flow analysis in this section, you will know exactly how much income you can expect to receive as well as nearly all the expenses you plan to cover with that income. (Don't plan on any sudden windfalls, but do expect a few surprise expenses.)

Roadmap 1.6, the Cash Flow Worksheet, is designed to be used annually. Some income, such as bonuses or capital gains distributions made by mutual funds, is received only at certain times of the year—for example, in December. Similarly, many expenses, such as tuition payments, fuel oil bills, or quarterly tax bills, occur only during certain months of the year. By totaling all your annual income and expenses, you will get a sense of how your overall cash flow looks for the year.

It is also important to do a more short-term cash flow analysis because sometimes you can get into a cash squeeze when your expenses are due before the income arrives. The same Cash Flow Worksheet in Roadmap 1.6 can be filled out on both a monthly and a quarterly basis.

We have designed this worksheet to be as comprehensive as possible, providing you with lines for the most common sources of income and the most frequent expenses, broken down into familiar categories. If you currently do not have one of the sources of income listed, leave the lines blank. The same holds true on the expense side. If you are not spending money for day care or a health club membership, leave it blank.

The best way to complete this worksheet is to take your bank, brokerage, insurance, and other statements, last year's tax return, along with your last year-end paycheck or W-2 and other records you have accumulated for the past six months, and fill in the real numbers. This is not an exercise in wishful thinking; this is a map that will show you, for better or worse, how

Roadmap 1.6

Cash Flow Worksheet

Annual Income	$ Amount	$ Total
1. Earned Income		
Salary after Tax Deductions	$_____	
Bonuses	_____	
Commissions	_____	
Deferred Compensation Proceeds	_____	
Overtime	_____	
Stock Option Proceeds	_____	
Tips	_____	
Other	_____	
Total Earned Income		$_____
2. Self-Employment Income		
Freelance Income	$_____	
Income from Partnerships	_____	
Income from Running a Small Business	_____	
Rental Income from Real Estate	_____	
Royalties	_____	
Other	_____	
Total Self-employment Income		$_____
3. Family Income		
Alimony Income	$_____	
Child Support Income	_____	
Family Trust Income	_____	
Gifts from Family Members	_____	
Inheritance Income	_____	
Other	_____	
Total Family Income		$_____
4. Government Income		
Aid to Families with Dependent Children	$_____	
Disability Insurance Income	_____	
Unemployment Insurance Income	_____	
Veterans Benefits	_____	
Welfare Income	_____	
Workers' Compensation Income	_____	

Other _____

Total Government Income $_____

5. Retirement Income
Annuity Payments $_____
Social Security Income   _____
Pension Income   _____
Income from IRAs   _____
Income from Keogh Accounts   _____
Income from Profit-Sharing Accounts   _____
Income from Salary Reduction Plans   _____
(401(k), 403(b), 457 plans)
Other   _____

Total Retirement Income $_____

6. Investment Income
Bank Account Interest
  CDs $_____
  Money-Market Accounts   _____
  NOW Accounts   _____
  Saving Accounts   _____
Bonds and Bond Funds
  Capital Gains   _____
  Dividends   _____
  Interest   _____
  Other   _____
Limited Partnerships (real estate,
oil, gas)   _____
Money Funds and T-Bills
  Taxable Funds   _____
  Tax-Exempt Funds   _____
  T-Bills   _____
Stock and Stock Funds
  Capital Gains   _____
  Dividends   _____
  Interest   _____
  Other   _____
Other   _____

Total Investment Income $_____

7. Other Income (specify)
_____ $_____

Total Other Income $_____
Total Annual Income $_____

Annual Expenses	$ Amount	$ Total
1. Fixed Expenses		
Automobile-Related	$_____	
Car Payment (loan or lease)	_____	
Gasoline or Oil	_____	
Other	_____	
Total		$_____
Family		
Alimony	_____	
Child Support Payments	_____	
Food and Beverage	_____	
School Tuition	_____	
Other	_____	
Total		$_____
Home-Related		
Mortgage Payments Home #1	_____	
Mortgage Payments Home #2	_____	
Rent	_____	
Total		$_____
Insurance		
Auto	_____	
Disability	_____	
Dental	_____	
Health	_____	
Homeowners	_____	
Life	_____	
Other	_____	
Total		$_____
Bank Loan Repayment		$_____
Savings and Investments		
Emergency Fund Contributions	_____	
Salary Reduction Plans Contributions (401(k), 403(b), 457 plans)	_____	
Other	_____	
Total		$_____
Taxes		
Federal	_____	
State	_____	
Local	_____	
Property	_____	
Social Security (self-employed)	_____	

Other	_____	
Total		$_____
Utilities		
Electricity	_____	
Gas	_____	
Telephone	_____	
Cable	_____	
Water and Sewage	_____	
Other	_____	
Total		$_____
Other (specify)		
_____	_____	
Total		$_____
Total Fixed Expenses		$_____

2. Flexible Expenses

Children		
Allowances	$_____	
Babysitting	_____	
Books	_____	
Camp Fees	_____	
Day Care	_____	
Events (parties, class trips, etc.)	_____	
Toys	_____	
Other	_____	
Total		$_____
Clothing		
New Purchases	_____	
Shoes	_____	
Upkeep (cleaning, tailoring, dry cleaning, etc.)	_____	
Total		$_____
Contributions and Dues		
Charitable Donations	_____	
Gifts (Christmas, birthdays, etc.)	_____	
Political Contributions	_____	
Religious Contributions	_____	
Union Dues	_____	
Other	_____	
Total		$_____
Education		
Room and Board	_____	
Books and Supplies (parents and/or children)	_____	

Annual Expenses	$ Amount	$ Total
Tuition (parents and/or children)	_____	
Other	_____	
Total		$_____
Equipment and Vehicles		
Appliance Purchases and Maintenance	_____	
Car, Boat, and Other Vehicle Purchases and Maintenance	_____	
Computer Purchases, etc.	_____	
Consumer Electronics Purchases	_____	
Licenses and Registration of Cars, Boats, etc.	_____	
Parking	_____	
Other	_____	
Total		$_____
Financial and Professional Services		
Banking Fees	_____	
Brokerage Commissions and Fees	_____	
Financial Advice	_____	
Legal Advice	_____	
Tax Preparation Fees	_____	
Other	_____	
Total		$_____
Food		
Groceries	_____	
Alcohol	_____	
Food and Snacks away from Home	_____	
Restaurant Meals	_____	
Tobacco	_____	
Other	_____	
Total		$_____
Home Maintenance		
Garbage Removal	_____	
Garden Supplies and Maintenance	_____	
Home Office Supplies	_____	
Home Furnishings	_____	
Home or Apartment Repairs and Renovations	_____	
Home Cleaning Services	_____	
Home Supplies	_____	
Lawn Care and Snow Removal	_____	
Linens	_____	
Uninsured Casualty or Theft Loss	_____	

Other	_____	
Total		$_____
Medical Care		
Dentist Bills	_____	
Drugs (over the counter)	_____	
Drugs (prescriptions)	_____	
Eye care and Eyeglasses	_____	
Hospital (uninsured portion)	_____	
Medical Devices (wheelchairs, canes, etc.)	_____	
Medical Expenses (parents, etc.)	_____	
Nursing Home Fees (parents, etc.)	_____	
Personal Beauty Care (hair stylist, manicurist, etc.)	_____	
Personal Care (cosmetics, toiletries, etc.)	_____	
Physician Bills	_____	
Unreimbursed Medical Expenses	_____	
Other	_____	
Total		$_____
Miscellaneous		
Mystery Cash	_____	
Postage and Stamps	_____	
Recurring Nonrecurring Expenses	_____	
Unreimbursed Business Expenses	_____	
Other	_____	
Total		$_____
Recreation and Entertainment		
Animal Care	_____	
Books	_____	
Club Dues	_____	
Cultural Events	_____	
Health Club Memberships	_____	
Hobbies	_____	
Lottery Tickets	_____	
Magazine and Newspaper Subscriptions	_____	
Movie Admissions	_____	
Music Admissions	_____	
Photography (cameras, developing, film, etc.)	_____	
Play Admissions	_____	
Recreational Equipment (games, sports, etc.)	_____	

Annual Expenses	$ Amount	$ Total
Sporting Events Admission	_____	
Videotape Rentals	_____	
Other	_____	
Total		$_____
Savings and Investments		
Bank Savings Contributions	_____	
Stock, Bond, and Mutual Fund Contributions	_____	
IRA Contributions	_____	
Keogh Account Contributions	_____	
Company-Sponsored Retirement Plan	_____	
Other	_____	
Total		$_____
Travel and Vacations		
Bus Fares	_____	
Subway Costs	_____	
Tolls	_____	
Train Fares	_____	
Travel Expenses (other than vacations)	_____	
Unreimbursed Business Travel Expenses	_____	
Vacations (airfare)	_____	
Vacations (car rental)	_____	
Vacations (food)	_____	
Vacations (hotel)	_____	
Vacations (other)	_____	
Other	_____	
Total		$_____
Other (specify)		
_____	_____	
Total		$_____
Total Flexible Expenses		$_____
Total Annual Expenses (Fixed + Flexible)		$_____
Total Annual Income		$_____
(Minus)		
Total Annual Expenses		(_____)
(Equals)		
Total Net Annual Positive (or Negative) Cash Flow		$_____

you are actually earning and spending your money now, and what you have left over to reach your goals. It's no use inflating the income and low-balling the expenses because you're the only one who will be hurt by not knowing the truth.

After you've filled out both the income and expense sides of this worksheet, you need to get down to the bottom line. Subtract your expenses from your income, and you have your annual cash flow. If you are taking in more than you are spending, congratulations—you have achieved a positive cash flow! Your next job is to figure out the best places to put your extra cash—probably savings vehicles and investments—in order to meet your goals.

If, on the other hand, your expenses total more than your income—not an unlikely situation—you are in negative cash flow, and it's time to start scrutinizing your expenses. By the way, negative cash flow does not necessarily mean you are in trouble. For example, you may still be putting away money in your company savings plan, which means you are actually saving money toward some goal—probably retirement. If, however, the reason you are spending more than you are taking in is excessive debt, it's time to take notice. This is a loud wake-up call telling you that now is the time to mend your ways, and alerting you to create a financial plan and budget that will help you meet your goals.

▶ Budgeting to Reach Your Destination

Often, the word *budget* sounds constricting, foreboding, and even a bit frightening. Actually, you should see a budget as your friend. It is the document that gives you control over your finances—it lets you decide what is most and least important to you.

A budget is an intensely personal plan; there is probably no one you know who has exactly the same priorities you have. If a lavish ski vacation to the Alps every winter is a high priority, so be it—as long as the numbers tell you that you can afford it.

One family, for example, decided they wanted to purchase a new SUV for their camping trips, but they did not want to stop saving for their children's education. Instead they decided to cut back on other expenses—they did a lot more shopping at garage sales and auctions, bought fewer clothes, and resisted the temptation of eating out regularly. Each month without exception they invested $300 in the mutual fund they'd bought for the kids' education.

(More about mutual funds in Chapters 3 and 4.) As a result, in a year-and-a-half, this family of four with two young children saved what they needed for the car. The best part was the feeling of confidence they gained when they actually pulled out of the car dealer's lot knowing that they hadn't forsaken their goal to provide a college education for their children.

Once you become accustomed to budgeting, you will wonder how you got through all those years without one. A budget is a living, breathing document that expands or contracts as your circumstances change. It is indeed a roadmap, allowing you to know the direction you want to go in, but giving you several options for how to get there.

For example, you might be planning to buy a house in three years, and you are carefully putting aside money for a down payment. Then you are involved in a car accident that puts you out of work for six months. Your budget must change, causing your down payment plans to be put off for a while. This does not mean you will never buy the house, it only means that your budget priorities have had to adapt to altered circumstances.

Creating a written budget, therefore, accomplishes several tasks. It communicates your priorities in black and white and it is a much better way than counting those numbers on your fingertips. The process itself will motivate you to take charge of your financial life. It will help you know exactly whether you are saving or overspending. At the end of the year, you would be in a good position to assess yourself and make a better budget for the coming year.

As you make out your budget (see Roadmap 1.7), keep in mind a few common sense tips:

1. A budget takes thought, so you probably can't do a good job of forecasting all your income and expenses in an afternoon. Plan to do it in several sessions over about a week's time.
2. Work out a budget with everyone who will be affected by it. A budget should not be engraved in stone. Instead, it should be discussed with your spouse and children so they feel involved in the planning and committed to its success. This way, you have a much better chance of meeting your targets than if your family members provided no input.
3. Be realistic and specific to your situation. You should not count on levels of spending or income that you only wish you had, or that your neighbor has. That will only frustrate the exercise. Also, remember that a budget, in itself, will not increase your income or cut your spending; it only allows you to see what is going on so that you can improve it.

Roadmap 1.7

Annual Budgeting Worksheet

Year _____

Annual Income	Actual Last Year	Budget This Year	Actual This Year	+/(−) Budget vs. Actual This Year
Earned Income	$_____	$_____	$_____	$_____
Self-Employment Income	_____	_____	_____	_____
Family Income	_____	_____	_____	_____
Government Income	_____	_____	_____	_____
Retirement Income	_____	_____	_____	_____
Investment Income	_____	_____	_____	_____
Other Income	_____	_____	_____	_____
Total Annual Income	$_____	$_____	$_____	$_____
Expenses				
Fixed Expenses				
Automobile-Related	$_____	$_____	$_____	$_____
Family	_____	_____	_____	_____
Home-Related	_____	_____	_____	_____
Insurance	_____	_____	_____	_____
Savings and Investments	_____	_____	_____	_____
Taxes	_____	_____	_____	_____
Utilities	_____	_____	_____	_____
Other	_____	_____	_____	_____
Total Fixed Expenses	$_____	$_____	$_____	$_____
Flexible Expenses				
Children	$_____	$_____	$_____	$_____
Clothing	_____	_____	_____	_____
Contributions and Dues	_____	_____	_____	_____
Education	_____	_____	_____	_____
Equipment and Vehicles	_____	_____	_____	_____
Financial and Professional Services	_____	_____	_____	_____
Food	_____	_____	_____	_____
Home Maintenance	_____	_____	_____	_____
Medical Care	_____	_____	_____	_____
Miscellaneous	_____	_____	_____	_____
Recreation and Entertainment	_____	_____	_____	_____
Savings and Investments	_____	_____	_____	_____
Travel and Vacations	_____	_____	_____	_____
Other	_____	_____	_____	_____
Total Flexible Expenses	$_____	$_____	$_____	$_____
Total Expenses	$_____	$_____	$_____	$_____
Total Income Less Total Expenses	$_____	$_____	$_____	$_____

4. When setting priorities, refer back to Roadmap 1.4, where you decided which goals were most and least important to you.

5. When making projections for the next year, don't automatically assume you will earn or spend the same amount in each category as you did the previous year. Last year's figures should be a guide, not a straitjacket. Part of your budget is taking control of your finances, so move numbers on the expense side up or down, depending—to some extent—on what you would like to see happen in the next year.

In setting up your budget (see Roadmap 1.7), enter the totals from Roadmap 1.6 in the first column, "Actual Last Year." Record what you actually earned and spent in each of the categories in the past year. This should be easy because all you have to do is transfer the figures from the Cash Flow Worksheet.

Next, you want to project what you think you will earn and what you want to spend in each of the categories over the next year, and enter the amounts in the second column, "Budget This Year." As you proceed through the year, you will be keeping track of what you are *actually* earning and spending in each category and these numbers should be entered in the third column, "Actual This Year." In the fourth column, you will calculate whether you are above or below what you projected in each category.

By doing this, you can instantly see whether your income and expenses are over or under your projected figures. When you total them, you would know whether you are above or below your total budget. If you are over budget, the culprit category usually sticks out like a sore thumb. If you are under budget, you might make a mid-course correction to see where else you can put some money, such as in savings or investments toward college.

In addition to doing an annual budget, you should keep a running tab on your monthly expenses at least in the major categories. You can modify Roadmap 1.7 for this purpose. Again, you should compare your budgeted amount with your actual income and spending. At the end of the worksheet, calculate whether you are over or under budget overall. Using this worksheet, you will be able to see month by month what kind of progress you are making toward meeting your budget and what items are at the greatest variance with your projections. By now, you have assembled a pretty accurate picture of where you stand financially.

You have clearly prioritized your financial goals, and you have analyzed how your income matches up with your expenses. With time on your side, small amounts of money saved regularly for 10 to 40 years will grow tremendously, and if you pay attention to how you invest your money, it will grow even more.

Map Your Route

Financing the Trip to College

Okay. You've decided that saving for your child's education is high on your medium- to long-range priority list, and you know that this is a long and potentially costly trip, but you also know that it has never been more worthwhile to attend college. So, how are you going to get there?

▶ How Much Will this Trip Cost?
Estimating College Costs

Let's start with what we know now. The average nationwide cost of college attendance (tuition and fees, not including room and board) for the 2003–04 school year was $19,710 for a four-year private college and $4,694 for a four-year public university for an in-state resident (*Trends in College Pricing, 2003*, by the College Board). Add about $7,000 if your child attends an out-of-state public university, for a total of $11,740. Multiply the national average annual cost by four years, and it costs anywhere from $18,776 (for a public university) to $78,840 (for a private college) just for the tuition and books for one child for four years of college today, not including annual price increases or room and board. If you and your child set your sights on an Ivy League school, the price ranges from $100,000 to $150,000.

During the 2003–04 school year, the average public university tuition and fees increased 14.1 percent; private college costs rose 6 percent. Historically, college costs have climbed at about twice the annual inflation rate. Currently, college costs are expected to increase between 4 and 7 percent a year, which means today's prices could look like bargains 20 years from now. For example, unless the pace of college cost inflation dramatically (and unexpectedly) slows, parents of a baby born in 1998 should expect to pay a whopping $100,000 to $150,000 for their child's public education and a mind-boggling $300,000 to $400,000 for four years at a top-ranked private university.

Therefore, if your child is born today, and if college costs increase by, let's say, an average of 5 percent per year for the next 18 years, the projected cost of a year at a public university is about $30,000. Based on a 6 percent return on your investments, you would need to save about $320 per month for the next 18 years to fund four years at a public university. For a private college, the cost in 18 years will be about $67,000, more than doubling your needed monthly savings to almost $700. Of course, these estimates are based on today's average costs—individual college costs could vary significantly, requiring you to save more or possibly less.

As you can see, how much you need primarily depends on the choice of college and its costs (including tuition, books, room and board, living expenses, etc.), the anticipated increase in the cost until your child reaches college age, and—something we haven't yet talked about—the likelihood of your child receiving financial aid. The good news is that many students receive some sort of financial aid. The not so good news is that most of the financial aid is in the form of loans, very few of which pay the full cost (see Chapter 6).

Perhaps, you're thinking, you'll never make this trip, but don't forget that millions of people finance their children's college education, and you can be one of them. It will take long-term saving and investing (see Chapters 3, 4, and 5) in the years before your child enters college. Once your child enrolls, you would probably have to try to help support them out of your current cash flow and/or take out loans—but we will come to all that later. Remember, the more prestigious the school your child goes to, the more it will cost, and the more you will have to save or borrow to meet tuition. Many excellent schools charge far less tuition than Ivy League universities, though they may not have the prestigious reputation. Sending your child to one of these less expensive institutions may ease some of the financial pressure. And for most people, it matters little from which institution we graduate, but rather that we graduated.

Most parents save far less than they ultimately need for college costs, so if you can motivate yourself to invest more, you will be that much closer to your goal. After all, what's the worst that could happen if you save too much? In the unlikely event that you accumulate more than enough money for college tuition, room, board, and other expenses, such as books and transportation, you will have plenty of other uses for the assets—like your retirement, for instance. However, if you save too little, you and your child will be forced to assume debt that will take years to repay and cost thousands of dollars in interest.

So, let's mosey on down the road, and instead of dwelling on the hundreds of thousands of dollars that college *could* cost, let's begin by seeing where you are now financially. You need to calculate how much you might *really* pay and how much you'll need to save for that education.

▶ Where Are You Now?

You now know your destination and have a rough idea of what it will cost; you've calculated your income and how much you spend. You've created a budget but to complete your financial picture, you must take stock of where you are right now; that is, you must compute your net worth.

Calculating your net worth is like weighing in at the airport before taking off on a round-the-world flight. To find out what your stuff weighs, you add up the total value of what you already own, known as your *assets,* and subtract the amount of any debt you owe, known as your *liabilities.* This bottom line is known as your *net worth.* It is a snapshot in time, good only for the moment you calculate it. Consider this photo the first in a lifelong album of financial achievements. Your first statement gives you a benchmark to compare yourself against as your net worth grows over the years.

By doing this exercise, you will be able to see clearly how your assets and liabilities match (or mismatch). As you find ways to control your spending, pay off your debts, and increase your savings and investment assets, you can make your net worth grow, which, in turn, will permit you to reach your financial goals. If you are doing all the wrong things, like increasing your debt and depleting your savings, this will show up quickly in your net worth as well.

Calculating your net worth is also important because it lets you see at a glance whether you are accumulating enough assets to support yourself comfortably in retirement. In addition, a current net worth statement will come in handy when you apply for loans or for financial aid for your children's college education, because lenders will require you to show your assets and liabilities on the application.

Before You Leave Home Give Yourself a Financial Checkup

As a rule, you should compute your net worth once a year to track how you're doing, and when there has been a major change in your financial situation. That might mean when you become eligible to receive an employee benefit like a pension, when you buy a home or car, when you contribute to a Keogh or an individual retirement account (IRA), or when your Aunt Sally dies and leaves you a big inheritance.

Assets. There are five classes of assets. What distinguishes one kind from another is how quickly you can turn it into cash or, put another way, how *liquid* it is. The more liquid an asset, the easier it is to put a value on it. For instance, you know exactly what the $102.55 in your checking account is worth, but you would probably have to ask a local real estate agent or appraiser to give you an estimate of the current worth of your home. Because of the different levels of liquidity of different assets, we suggest that you separate your assets into these five classes:

Current assets. Current assets are easily convertible into cash; for instance, bank accounts, money-market mutual funds, and Treasury securities. For each of these you own, list the name of the bank where the asset is held, the balance, and the current yield. Also, list the yield on Treasury bills, which mature in a year or less, and U.S. savings bonds, which you can cash in any time as long as you have held them for at least six months. If you have overpaid your taxes and are due a refund from the Internal Revenue Service (IRS) or your state tax department, you should also count that as a current asset. If you are owed a bonus or commission within the next few months, that counts as current, too.

Securities. These include publicly traded stocks, bonds, mutual funds, and so on. The current market values of all such securities are available in most major newspapers, particularly *The Wall Street Journal,* as well as from your broker or from stock quotation services, such as http://finance.yahoo.com.

For each security, list your purchase price, the number of units held (such as number of shares of stock), the percentage yield it pays (a dividend for a stock, interest for a bond), when it matures (for a bond, a futures contract, or an option), and the balance.

Real estate. Real estate includes first and second homes, condominiums, cooperatives, rental properties, and real estate limited partnerships. The current worth of all real estate should be based on appraisals from knowledgeable local experts like appraisers or estimates from real estate agents. Remember to subtract all selling costs, such as the standard real estate broker's commission, and the amount due on any mortgage. For partnerships, list the yield being paid to you, if any, and the year you expect the partnership to be liquidated and the proceeds paid out to you. Also include any mortgage loans that may be due to you, such as on a house you sold on which you were granted a loan.

Long-term assets. These include the cash value of life insurance policies; the worth of annuities, pensions, and profit-sharing plans; IRAs and Keogh plans; any long-term loans due to you; any long-term royalties due to you from writing a book or having patented an invention that is still selling; and any interests you have in an ongoing business.

Long-term assets are often difficult to value because you have access to their true worth only several years, or even decades, from now. Still, your life insurance company can tell you the current cash value of policies and annuities, and your employer will tell you what your pension and profit-sharing plans would be worth if you left the company now. Valuing your interest in a closely held business is particularly tricky, but it can be done.

Personal property. Personal property such as cars, jewelry, collectibles, and home furnishings would be valued at whatever you think they could be sold for now in their present condition. In valuing personal property, try to be as realistic as possible. Don't just put down what you think they are worth; this number is often inflated. You should try to get some sense of the market when you value things. For instance, check with a used-car dealer, the used-car ads in your newspaper, or the *National Automobile Dealers Association Blue Book* (http://www.nadaguides.com) or http://www.edmunds.com to see what your car's model and year is now worth. Bring any rare coins or stamps into a reputable dealer for an appraisal. For antiques or other collectibles, contact a local member of the American Society of Appraisers, found in the Yellow Pages, or have a look at eBay.

In the Assets Worksheet in Roadmap 2.1, make a detailed list of not only the assets you have but also who holds the titles to them. If you are married,

Roadmap 2.1

Assets Worksheet

Assets	Date Purchased	Original $ Cost	Current Date	Current $ Value
1. Current Assets				
Bonuses or Commissions (due you)	_____	$_____	_____	$_____
Certificates of Deposit	_____	_____	_____	_____
	_____	_____	_____	_____
Checking Accounts	_____	_____	_____	_____
	_____	_____	_____	_____
Credit Union Accounts	_____	_____	_____	_____
Money-Market Accounts	_____	_____	_____	_____
	_____	_____	_____	_____
Savings Accounts	_____	_____	_____	_____
	_____	_____	_____	_____
Savings Bonds	_____	_____	_____	_____
	_____	_____	_____	_____
Tax Refunds (due you)	_____	_____	_____	_____
Treasury Bills	_____	_____	_____	_____
Total Current Assets		$_____		$_____
2. Securities				
Bonds (type of bond)				
_____	_____	$_____	_____	$_____
_____	_____	_____	_____	_____
_____	_____	_____	_____	_____
_____	_____	_____	_____	_____
Bond Mutual Funds				
_____	_____	_____	_____	_____
_____	_____	_____	_____	_____
Individual Stocks				
_____	_____	_____	_____	_____
_____	_____	_____	_____	_____
_____	_____	_____	_____	_____
_____	_____	_____	_____	_____
_____	_____	_____	_____	_____
Stock Mutual Funds				
_____	_____	_____	_____	_____
_____	_____	_____	_____	_____
_____	_____	_____	_____	_____
_____	_____	_____	_____	_____
Futures Contracts	_____	_____	_____	_____
Warrants and Options	_____	_____	_____	_____
Total Securities		$_____		$_____

Assets	Date Purchased	Original $ Cost	Current Date	Current $ Value
3. Real Estate				
Mortgage Receivable (due you)	___	$ ___	___	$ ___
Primary Residence	___	___	___	___
Rental Property	___	___	___	___
Real Estate Limited Partnerships	___	___	___	___
Second Home	___	___	___	___
Total Real Estate		$ ___		$ ___
4. Long-Term Assets				
Annuities	___	$ ___	___	$ ___
IRAs	___	___	___	___
Keogh Accounts	___	___	___	___
Life Insurance Cash Values	___	___	___	___
Loans Receivable (due you)	___	___	___	___
Pensions	___	___	___	___
Private Business Interests	___	___	___	___
Profit-Sharing Plans	___	___	___	___
Royalties	___	___	___	___
Salary Reduction Plans (401(k), 403(b), 457 plans)	___	___	___	___
Total Long-term Assets		$ ___		$ ___
5. Personal Property				
Antiques	___	$ ___	___	$ ___
Appliances (washing machines, dishwashers, vacuum cleaners, etc.)	___	___	___	___
Automobiles	___	___	___	___
Boats, etc.	___	___	___	___
Campers, Trailers, etc.	___	___	___	___
Clothing	___	___	___	___
Coin Collections	___	___	___	___
Computers, etc.	___	___	___	___
Furniture	___	___	___	___
Furs	___	___	___	___
Home Entertainment Equipment (CD players, stereos, televisions, VCRs, etc.)	___	___	___	___
Home Furnishings (drapes, blankets, etc.)	___	___	___	___

Jewelry	_____	_____	_____	_____
Lighting Fixtures	_____	_____	_____	_____
Motorcycles, etc.	_____	_____	_____	_____
Paintings and Sculptures	_____	_____	_____	_____
Pools, etc.	_____	_____	_____	_____
Stamp Collections	_____	_____	_____	_____
Tableware (glasses, plates, silverware, etc.)	_____	_____	_____	_____
Tools, etc.				
Other				
Total Personal Property	$ _____		$ _____	
Total Assets	$ _____		$ _____	

you can own property jointly or separately. Some assets, like a securities portfolio for a child, may be held in a trust for which the parents are responsible until the child turns 18. If you need more space for any category as you fill out the worksheets, copy that page and attach it to your worksheet.

Liabilities. Liabilities, or what you owe others, are not as much fun to add up as assets, but you've got to add them up anyway. Just like the assets, liabilities should also be divided into short- and long-term categories. That's because some debts, like current bills or credit cards, need to be paid back very soon, while other debts, like mortgages or college loans, will take years to repay. In Roadmap 2.2 Liabilities Worksheet, list those to whom you owe money, the interest rate you are paying, if any, when the loan comes due if there is such a maturity date, and how much money you owe. You should use the following four main categories for listing your liabilities:

Current liabilities. These are debts you must pay within the next six months. In this category would be bills from the utilities (the telephone company, the electric company, the gas company, and the oil company), physicians and dentists, home repair contractors, retail stores, and other short-term creditors. You should also include regular alimony or child support payments if these apply to you. If you owe money to a relative or friend who helped you out in a pinch, make sure to also include that debt in this category.

Unpaid taxes. These taxes might be due either on April 15 or as part of your quarterly estimated tax payments to both the IRS and your state tax

Roadmap 2.2

Liabilities Worksheet

Liabilities	To Whom	Interest Rate %	Due Date	Amount Due $
1. Current Liabilities				
Alimony	_____	_____ %	_____	$ _____
Bills				
Electric & Gas	_____	_____	_____	_____
Home Contractor	_____	_____	_____	_____
Oil Company	_____	_____	_____	_____
Physician & Dentist	_____	_____	_____	_____
Retail Stores	_____	_____	_____	_____
Telephone	_____	_____	_____	_____
Other	_____	_____	_____	_____
Child Support	_____	_____	_____	_____
Loans to Individuals	_____	_____	_____	_____
Total Current Liabilities				$ _____
2. Unpaid Taxes				
Income Taxes				
Federal	_____	_____ %	_____	$ _____
State	_____	_____	_____	_____
City	_____	_____	_____	_____
Capital Gains Taxes				
Federal	_____	_____	_____	_____
State	_____	_____	_____	_____
City	_____	_____	_____	_____
Property Taxes	_____	_____	_____	_____
Sales Taxes Locality	_____	_____	_____	_____
Social Security Taxes (self-employed)	_____	_____	_____	_____
Total Unpaid Taxes				$ _____
3. Real Estate Liabilities				
Home #1				
First Mortgage	_____	_____ %	_____	$ _____
Second Mortgage	_____	_____	_____	_____
Home Equity Loan	_____	_____	_____	_____
Home #2				
First Mortgage	_____	_____	_____	_____
Second Mortgage	_____	_____	_____	_____
Home Equity Loan	_____	_____	_____	_____
Rental Property				
First Mortgage	_____	_____	_____	_____
Second Mortgage	_____	_____	_____	_____
Total Real Estate Liabilities				$ _____

4. Installment Liabilities

Automobile Loans	_____	_____ %	_____	$ _____
Loans for Bill Consolidation	_____	_____	_____	_____
Credit Cards	_____	_____	_____	_____
Education Loans	_____	_____	_____	_____
Equipment and Appliance Loans	_____	_____	_____	_____
Furniture Loans	_____	_____	_____	_____
Home Improvement Loans	_____	_____	_____	_____
Liability Judgments	_____	_____	_____	_____
Life Insurance Loans	_____	_____	_____	_____
Margin Loans	_____	_____	_____	_____
Overdraft Bank Loans	_____	_____	_____	_____
Retirement Plan Loans	_____	_____	_____	_____
Other Loans	_____	_____	_____	_____
Total Installment Liabilities				$ _____
Total Liabilities				$ _____

department. They include not only income taxes but also the capital gains taxes you owe on an asset you have sold for a profit. You should also include local property taxes, which you may have to pay directly, or which may be paid by the company that holds your mortgage. Finally, if you are self-employed, you must make sure to account for Social Security self-employment taxes due.

Real estate debt. This category of debt includes both first and second mortgages on your primary residence and on any second (or even third, if you should be so lucky) home you may have. It also includes any mortgages you owe on rental properties that are producing income. On a separate line, list any home equity loans outstanding on your first or second home.

Installment debt. Installment debt covers all loans you have committed to pay off over a period of time. This category includes automobile loans from either a car dealer or a bank; loans taken out to consolidate bills or for any other purpose including overdraft loans attached to your checking account; education loans from your college or university; loans to pay for equipment or appliances, including computers; furniture loans; home improvement loans; life insurance loans taken against the cash value in your policies; and margin loans from a brokerage house taken against the value of your securities. If you have lost a lawsuit and there is a liability judgment against you, that should be considered part of the installment debt you owe.

Finally, if you have borrowed against your retirement plan at work, which is usually some form of salary reduction plan, you normally are obligated to pay it back by payroll deduction over five years. This obligation should also be counted as installment debt. Credit card charges from MasterCard, Visa, American Express, Diners Club, and Discover, as well as retail stores, on which you owe at least the minimum payment should also be noted in this category because you control when to pay off the outstanding balance.

Now, for the moment of truth: Take your total assets from Roadmap 2.1 and subtract your total liabilities from Roadmap 2.2. This determines your net worth.

Total Assets	$ _____
(Minus) Total Liabilities	(_____)
Equals Positive (or Negative) Net Worth	$ _____

First, notice whether your net worth is positive or negative. If it's positive, you've probably been doing a good job at building assets and keeping liabilities under control. Now that you know where you stand, you are in a good position to see your net worth grow even more in coming years, and you should be on your way to funding your child's education.

If your net worth is negative, do not despair. You have just discovered something very important about your finances. Knowing that you are under water (financially speaking) is the first step in getting out of trouble. Clearly, you have too much debt for the amount of assets you have accumulated. Remember, this is only a snapshot of your current situation. Let's hope the next time you calculate your net worth, it will be a more "positive" experience.

After you calculate your net worth each year, compare it to your calculations for the preceding five years to see how you have been progressing. If you've never done this exercise before, begin doing it now.

▶ When Does the Train Leave the Station?

The time horizon is the amount of time needed until you begin to use some or all of your investments. For example, if you plan to save for a down payment on a new house in two years, your investment time horizon is two years. If you're saving for a child's first year of college and that child is currently 10 years old, your investment time horizon is eight years (when the child is 18 and ready for college). The most important thing is to begin saving, even if it's $25 a month. As your income increases and/or you pay down debt, boost the amount you save.

How Long Do You Have Before the First Bill Comes Due?

Roadmap 2.3 will help you estimate your child's college costs and your savings needs. It assumes that your child will enter college at age 18, that you will continue to save throughout your child's college years, and that education costs will escalate 7 percent a year. We are also assuming that you earn 7 percent per year after taxes on your investments. To complete the worksheet, it's helpful to know the current annual cost of a school your child might attend. For more information, visit http://www.collegeboard.com.

Sample figures in Roadmap 2.3 are based on a college cost of $10,000 per year and a six-year-old child. For a rough idea of how much college might *actually* cost based on your child's current age, and how much you must save, ask your financial planner to calculate the amounts. You can also do it yourself by using relevant software or the many calculators on college financing Web sites listed in Appendix B of this book. (A similar exercise is available in *Quicken* and *Microsoft Money* and other software packages.) In most of these calculators, you enter the number of years until your child starts college, your assumed inflation rate, your estimated return on investments, and other factors to arrive at the expected college costs. As you change your assumptions, note how the cost of college and the amount you must save change. If you have more than one child, make sure you do these calculations for each child.

As you will see by trying various combinations of factors on the worksheet, the earlier you start to save, the less you must put aside each month or each year. And, of course, the longer you wait, the more you must save every month. As a rule of thumb, set aside between $2,000 and $4,000 a year if you begin when your child is a newborn. If you start saving when your child is in second or third grade, reserve between $4,000 and $8,000 a year. To give you an idea of how much money you will accumulate if you save $100 a month, use Roadmap 2.4. Find the number of years until your child enrolls in college in the left column. Across the top, you can see how your money

Roadmap 2.3

College Costs and Savings Needs Worksheet

	Example (assumes 7% return)	Your Child
1. Current Annual College Costs	$10,000	$_____
2. Age of Your Child	6	_____
3. Future Cost of First Year of College (Multiply item 1, above, by number in column A next to your child's age, below.)	$22,520	$_____
4. Total Cost of Four Years of College (Amount needed at the beginning of college. Multiply item 3 by 3.624.)	$81,626	$_____
5. Amount You Must Save or Invest Each Year (Multiply item 4 by number in column B next to your child's age.)	$4,563	$_____
6. Amount You Must Save or Invest Each Month (Divide item 5 by 12.)	$380	$_____

Age of Child	A	B
Newborn	3.380	0.0294
1	3.159	0.0324
2	2.952	0.0359
3	2.759	0.0398
4	2.579	0.0443
5	2.410	0.0496
6	2.252	0.0559
7	2.105	0.0634
8	1.967	0.0724
9	1.838	0.0835
10	1.718	0.0975
11	1.606	0.1155
12	1.501	0.1398
13	1.403	0.1739
14	1.311	0.2252
15	1.225	0.3110
16	1.145	0.4831
17	1.070	1.0000

Roadmap 2.4

Money Accumulated by Investing $100 Per Month

# of Years Until College	After-Tax Rates of Return		
	5.5%	7%	8%
1	$ 1,236	$ 1,246	$ 1,253
2	2,542	2,583	2,611
3	3,922	4,016	4,081
4	5,380	5,553	5,673
5	6,920	7,201	7,397
6	8,546	8,968	9,264
7	10,265	10,863	11,286
8	12,080	12,895	13,476
9	13,998	15,073	15,848
10	16,024	17,409	18,417
11	18,164	19,914	21,198
12	20,425	22,602	24,211
13	22,814	25,481	27,474
14	25,537	28,569	31,008
15	28,002	31,881	34,835
16	30,818	35,432	38,979
17	33,793	39,240	43,468
18	36,936	48,323	48,329

will compound at different after-tax rates of return. If you save more than $100 a month, multiply these numbers by the appropriate multiple of $100. For example, if you save $400 a month, multiply these numbers by four.

The sooner you begin saving, the better. As we said, very few families actually save the full amount needed to pay for college. Colleges generally expect that you will save about one-third of the required amount, borrow one-third, and fund another third from your cash flow while your child is in college.

▶ Itinerary: Assembling a Long-Term Financial Plan

While budgeting is crucial to balancing your income and spending over the coming months and years, you also have to take steps to project how your needs will evolve during the rest of your life. This process not only helps you avoid or at least be prepared for financial surprises and disasters; it helps those in good financial shape be better prepared for the future.

As you know by now, there are short-, medium-, and long-term dimensions to your financial life. While budgeting is aimed at satisfying your short-term goals, you might never get to the medium and long-term objectives without a financial plan. What follows is a brief introduction to the things you will need to consider in setting up your strategy for long-term success, particularly as it relates to funding your child's higher education.

Your financial plan will outline how much capital you will need to accumulate to meet certain long-term goals, such as paying for your children's college education, buying or upgrading a home, and providing for a secure retirement. Part of your investment strategy will include assembling a portfolio of stocks, bonds, mutual funds, and bank instruments that will get you where you want to go.

One of the main risks you must overcome in a long-term plan is the slow but steady erosion of the worth of a dollar because of inflation. A good investment strategy will keep your dollars growing faster than inflation so that by the time you need to spend them, you will have enough. Another element of investing is finding a level of risk with which you feel comfortable.

To accumulate the $50,000 to $100,000 or more that it will take to put each of your children through four years of college, you would have had to start planning—and saving—as soon as they were born. This takes a discipline that will pay off as they approach their freshman year. As we've seen, the later you start saving, the more you will need to invest each year to end up with the same college kitty.

In addition, it takes advance planning to understand and qualify for various kinds of student loan programs, both those offered by the government and individual schools. More details on college financing strategies can be found in the remaining chapters of this book.

Rise and Shine: The Advantages of an Early Start

The earlier you start saving for your child's education, the more time your money has to grow. The cost of a college education is one of the largest expenditures in raising children. Fortunately, several tax-advantaged options are available.

The best time to begin saving for your children's college education is before they are born. By implementing prudent budgeting techniques before your children are born, you should be able to accrue the necessary money to help you reach your financial goals. This is another example of how quantifying your goals can be put to use.

If you develop a realistic plan and commit seriously to it, you can meet most or all of the massive expenses. The earlier you develop a plan to fund college education, the easier it will be for you to handle this burden. If you ignore or put off the problem, the challenge of college funding becomes only more daunting, and you might not be able to help your children pay for college. While the sacrifice of saving for college may seem great, the reward can be even greater.

Know Before You Go

ABCs of Investing for College and Future Travel Plans

The higher the return you earn on your savings and investments, the less money you must set aside for your children's college tuition. Unfortunately, because no guarantees of high returns exist in the investment world without commensurate high risks, you should put together a balanced portfolio of high-, medium-, and low-risk investments to fund your children's college.

In general, the longer you have until you need the money, the more risk you can take in search of high returns. As the tuition bills draw closer and closer, you should take less and less risk. Ideally, all the money you need should sit in your money-market account on the day you write your first huge check.

▶ Adventure Travel or Quiet Drive in the Country: High Risk vs. Slow and Steady

For many people, the word *risk,* just like the word *budgeting,* has a negative connotation. "Why would I want to risk my hard-earned money?" you say. "I'm very conservative." The answer: If you take no risks with your assets, you will be unlikely to earn a return high enough to achieve your financial goals. A truism in the money world is "No risk, no return."

No, we're not advocating that you take enormous risks with all of your money. Not every risky investment will earn a high return; if it did, it wouldn't be risky. By diversifying your assets carefully among different types of investments, you are assured of ending up with a larger pool of assets over time than if you keep all of your money in low-risk, low-return choices.

In general, the further in the future a return is expected, the greater the risk. Because it is tricky enough to predict what is going to happen over the next few months, it is even more difficult to know what the long-term future holds. Therefore, under normal circumstances, the longer you commit yourself to an investment, the more risk you are taking. But because you are taking more risk, chances are that in the longer run you would be compensated with a higher return.

In order to determine your tolerance for risk, you should understand several types of risk. There are an enormous number of books written on ways to control and minimize each of these risks, but here we provide an overview of the most important risks you will face:

Currency risk. While most of your assets will probably be in dollar-denominated investments, you should be aware of the risk of currency movements if you own stocks or bonds or a mutual fund (more likely for most individuals) that invests in foreign securities. When you own a British stock, for example, your money has been converted into pounds. If the value of the pound falls against the U.S. dollar, your British shares will be worth less if you were to sell the stock and translate the pounds back into dollars; the opposite, of course, is also true.

Deflation risk. If prices are falling sharply, you face the risk that the value of your assets will drop drastically. Treasury bonds provide a good haven from deflation, for example, because it is safe to assume the government will always honor its obligations to bondholders.

Lack of diversification risk. If all your assets are in one type of investment, like stocks or bonds, you are not protected if that asset falls sharply in value. Even more dangerous is to keep most of your money in just one stock, bond, or mutual fund because if something happens to it, you have no other assets to fall back on. To lower this risk, spread your holdings among different types of assets as well as among several individual investments within each type of asset. One easy way to diversify is to buy a mutual fund, which itself holds dozens of stocks or bonds. We'll look at mutual funds later in this chapter.

Inflation risk. Sometimes you don't notice inflation risk until you must buy something you have not bought for several years and you are hit with sticker shock. For example, when you make your child's first tuition payment you may find yourself muttering: "Why, when I went to college, it cost me $5,000 for all four years, and now that covers only the first semester of freshman year!"

If you keep all your money in super safe CDs, money-market funds, and Treasuries, you run the risk of seeing your assets disappear in terms of buying power because your return has not kept up with inflation. This risk is not frequently recognized, but it is probably the biggest risk people take. By the time you have figured out that you have been too conservative with your investments, it is often too late to recover.

Interest rate risk. Interest-rate risk can cut both ways. If you lock into a fixed-rate instrument like a bond when rates are low, and then rates rise sharply, the value of your investment will plunge if you have to resell it. On the other hand, if your plan depends on the yields you can earn in an environment of high interest rates, you will endure a painful shock when rates fall.

Lack of marketability risk. What do you do when you need to sell something, but the market for it has dried up temporarily? You can hang on to it, or you can sell it even if you have to accept an artificially low price. In general, the more aggressive an investment is, the more subject it is to this type of risk. Stocks of small companies and junk bonds, for example, normally are relatively easy to buy and sell, but when bad news hits these markets or investors become nervous, the ability to sell at a fair price temporarily disappears.

Political risk. If you invest in countries where the political structure is unstable, a change in government might dramatically devalue the worth of your holdings. A milder form of political risk, which does affect American investments, is a change in government policy (legislation, tax policy, tariffs, subsidies, and so on) that favors one industry over another.

Repayment risk. There are two kinds of repayment risk. The most common, also known as credit risk, is the chance that you will not get repaid what you are owed when it is due because the borrower or bond issuer is unable to pay. Credit risk ratings by agencies such as Standard & Poor's and Moody's Investors Service, which range from AAA to D, will indicate the risk you are taking with a particular issue.

The second risk is that you are repaid *before* you want or expect to get your money back. Most bond issuers have the right to redeem (or *call,* as it is known) a bond a certain number of years after it has been issued. (One of the advantages of Treasury bonds is that they are usually noncallable.)

Volatility risk. This risk occurs when an investment swings wildly in value, up or down, in a short period of time. Of course, volatility gives you a greater chance to profit if you buy when the price is low and sell when it is high. But that's easier said than done, and many investors don't have the stomach for this ride. Just because an investment is volatile doesn't mean you should avoid it altogether, but you should realize what you've bought and be able to ride out sudden air pockets. Remember, you entered into the investment in the hope of long-term profits.

A Trip to Giza: The Investment Pyramid

In assembling a portfolio that both achieves your financial goals and still allows you to sleep comfortably at night, think of your entire mix of assets in the form of an investment pyramid as shown in Roadmap 3.1.

At the top of your pyramid are the riskiest assets, which offer the greatest potential for high returns as well as big losses. The high-risk apex includes collectibles, direct foreign investments, futures contracts, high yield corporate and municipal bonds, new stock issues, oil and gas limited partnerships, options, raw land, small growth stocks, tax shelters, unfinished real estate construction, venture capital, and warrants.

The next tier of the pyramid, the moderate-risk sector, includes stock and bond mutual funds, income-oriented limited partnerships, mortgage-backed securities, individual growth stocks, corporate bonds, and rental real estate.

The third tier of the pyramid, called the low-risk sector, consists of annuities, blue chip stocks, Treasury bonds, life insurance contracts, municipal bonds with high credit ratings, short-term bond funds, utility stocks, and zero-coupon bonds.

Roadmap 3.1

Investment Risk Levels

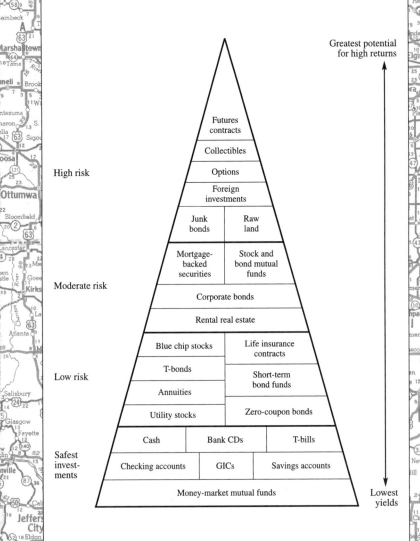

Greatest potential
for high returns

High risk

Futures
contracts

Collectibles

Options

Foreign
investments

Junk
bonds

Raw
land

Mortgage-
backed
securities

Stock and
bond mutual
funds

Moderate risk

Corporate bonds

Rental real estate

Low risk

Blue chip stocks

Life insurance
contracts

T-bonds

Short-term
bond funds

Annuities

Utility stocks

Zero-coupon bonds

Safest
invest-
ments

Cash

Bank CDs

T-bills

Checking accounts

GICs

Savings accounts

Money-market mutual funds

Lowest
yields

The base of the pyramid is composed of investments in which there is almost no chance of losing your principal. This includes bank CDs, cash, checking accounts, money-market mutual funds, and guaranteed investment contracts (GICs) found in many salary reduction plans, savings accounts, and Treasury bills. There is, as we mentioned, the risk of investments that are too safe. While your principal is not at risk, the investments earn low yields and therefore do not allow you to keep up with inflation.

How Long Before You Leave? Asset Allocation

Asset allocation is the process of determining which asset classes (stocks, real estate, bonds, cash, and more) should be represented, and in what proportions, in your investment portfolio. It's a critical part of the financial planning process but often is ignored in favor of sexier stock picking or a broker's hot *tip du jour.*

Research shows that more than 90 percent of the variation in investment returns among pension plan portfolios comes from the choice and weighting of asset classes, not from stock selection or market timing. Figuring out your portfolio's asset allocation depends on your unique circumstances, including age, time horizon, financial goals, and tolerance for investment risk. Allocation decisions can also be influenced by more transitory factors like market valuations, interest rates, and economic conditions. As circumstances change, your portfolio's asset mix will change over time, too.

At its core, asset allocation involves developing a formal investment strategy to achieve your financial objectives. It plays a critical role in your financial plan and provides a framework in which to make objective, unemotional portfolio decisions. It may not be the way to immediate, exceptional returns, but it is the proven way toward long-term wealth accumulation.

Your investment time horizon, or when the money will be needed, is important because of the risk or volatility of equities (stocks). Over the longer term, investors generally can assume more risk and thus allocate more of a portfolio to stocks. Tollbooth 3.1 is a guide—not a hard and fast rule, which depends on your needs and risk tolerance—to maximum stock (equity) exposure.

No matter what your age or situation, you should probably have some of your assets in each of the four sectors of the pyramid at all times. What should change over time is how much you invest in each sector. You might be young and able to take more risk, so more of your money should be in

Tollbooth 3.1

Time Horizon: Maximum Equity Allocation

0-3 years	0%	4-5 years	20%
6 years	30%	7 years	40%
8 years	50%	9 years	60%
10 years	70%	11+ years	80%

the high-risk apex. Nevertheless, you should still have a cash reserve in base investments.

All of this, of course, ultimately depends on your cash flow needs, time horizon, and risk tolerance; that is, how you feel and react when the value of your investments declines. For example, let's assume that you have allocated 70 percent of your portfolio to stocks and regularly add to your account, and suddenly in one year, you watched the bear market take 30 percent of your stocks' value. Can you continue to invest the new dollars needed to maintain your 70 percent allocation to equities, while at the same time watching the value of your portfolio go down?

History has shown that over longer periods of time (10 to 20 years) stocks outperform all other asset classes, so a well-thought-out investment plan can help you stay the course during the market's ups and downs. You want to avoid making emotion-based decisions that will hurt your portfolio's performance over the long run.

Finally, what are your financial objectives, and how much potential risk will you take to reach them? Sometimes, the amount of money you need drives the amount of risk or equity exposure you will take on. For example, if, based on the number of years you have until your child enters college, you need an 8 percent return on your investments, roughly 60 percent of your portfolio should be allocated to equities. Would you still be able to sleep at night while taking this kind of risk?

If the risk to achieve the return is more than you can stomach, but you don't want to reduce the amount of money you will contribute toward your child's education, consider saving more each month or decide to borrow more (or some combination of the two) to make up for the lower expected return that comes with taking less risk. Another alternative might be to investigate a work-study program (see Chapter 6).

▶ How Do You Want To Travel? Types of Investments

There are myriad things in which you can invest and there are innumerable books, newsletters, and Web sites telling you how to do it (you'll find some of the good ones listed in Appendix B: Resources). In the next three sections, we will examine some of the more popular forms of investments to give you an idea of what's available and how they fit both your risk profile and your goals; in particular, your goal of funding your child's education.

Highway 1: Stock Overview

If you've never invested in stocks or have only limited experience with them, you may believe that it's a dangerous, volatile place where thousands of sophisticated professional traders and brokers lurk to steal your hard-earned money. You may have heard scary stories of market crashes and how people's lifetime savings have vanished in a day.

The reality is that that view is just a myth. There are millions of average investors like you who have been able to finance their dreams by successfully buying and holding shares of profitable companies and of mutual funds. Millions of other investors depend on the regular income they earn from their stock and mutual fund holdings.

Sure, stock prices are volatile—they bob up and down—but if you look over the past few decades, prices of good-quality companies' stocks have invariably moved higher, as shareholders are rewarded by the performance of the stocks they own. As a device to increase your net worth so that you can achieve your financial goals, stocks or stock mutual funds have historically been your best investment over the long run.

Side Trips: Categories of Stocks

There are many types of stocks, and depending on your risk profile and financial objectives, some are more appropriate for you than others. As we travel the stock route, we'll take a look at the major categories to see how they fit your goal to fund your children's education as well as how they might complement your other goals.

Scenic View—Cyclical Stocks. The fortunes of certain companies are very closely tied to the ups and downs of the economy, and if you time purchases and sales of such company stocks well, you can profit handsomely. Cyclical stocks, so called because they ride the economic cycle, are typically found in such heavy industries as auto manufacturing, paper, chemicals, steel, and aluminum. All these companies have relatively large fixed costs to run their factories, so when the demand for their product is high and the prices they receive are rising, they can earn enormous profits. However, when demand is weak and prices are falling, they are still burdened by the same costs, and their earnings plummet.

Cyclical stock prices are even more volatile than the company's earnings. Investors are constantly trying to determine where we are in the economic cycle because it has a tremendous impact on the company's bottom line. While all stock prices reflect investors' expectations of future profits, cyclical stocks are even more sensitive to perceptions about the future, and trying to determine the right time to buy and sell is tricky, even for seasoned investors.

Mountain Aerie—Growth Stocks. Over the long term, you earn the highest return from stocks of growth companies with sharply rising earnings. Individual growth stocks pay few or no dividends because they reinvest most of their profits back in the business in an attempt to maintain or accelerate rapid growth.

The earnings of a true growth stock can compound at 15 percent or more no matter what the overall economy is doing. Growth stocks that perform well may offer exclusive, hot, niche products or services or have well-known brand names, strong finances, and top-flight management.

Sounds like a breeze, doesn't it? But it isn't! The better the record a growth company establishes, the higher investors' expectations soar and the higher the stock's price-earnings (P/E) ratio climbs. (The P/E ratio is the current price of a share of stock divided by its current earnings per share.) As long as the growth in earnings continues unabated, there are no problems, but the moment the company reports a slight slip in its upward trajectory, the stock can take a pounding.

A much safer and easier way to receive this type of growth opportunity is to invest in growth-oriented mutual funds. These funds often accept small amounts of money, such as $50 a month. Most important, professional fund managers attempt to buy the most promising growth stocks and sell the fading stars, so you should have a better chance of achieving maximum returns. Though such funds are volatile from month to month or year to year, chances are that a well-managed fund could provide an average annual return of 10 to 15 percent over the long term. Therefore, growth-oriented mutual funds can be very appropriate for the first 10 to 12 years of your child's life.

Rolling Hills—Income Stocks. While most people think of stocks as vehicles to achieve capital appreciation, they can also provide steady income in the form of quarterly dividends. Companies that pay high dividends usually are well-established, profitable firms. Some businesses that offer high-yielding stocks may include banking firms, real estate investment trusts, and electric, gas, and water utilities. Unlike faster growing younger companies, which reinvest profits in their own businesses, such firms traditionally pay out at least half their profits to shareholders in the form of dividends. Even more than prices of other stocks, high-yield stock prices are greatly influenced by changes in interest rates. When rates on Treasury bonds fall, high-yield stock prices tend to rise because that stock's dividends are more competitive with bonds. Conversely, when interest rates rise, high-yield stocks look less attractive and their prices tend to drop.

To make sure an income stock you are considering can continue to raise its dividend, analyze the company's debt to make sure it is financially strong. Debt that is more than 50 percent of the company's equity may be a sign of trouble. Another quick way to gauge financial strength is to check the stock's rating with a reputable credit rating agency's ratings, such as Standard & Poor's Stock Guide. Any rating over B+ implies that the company is financially solid.

The final ratio to inspect before you buy a stock for income is the payout ratio, the percentage of earnings that is paid out in dividends. A payout ratio consistently below 60 percent means that there is a sizable cushion for the company to fall back on before it has to cut its dividend. A low ratio also leaves room for the dividend to grow. On the other hand, a payout ratio consistently well above 60 percent might be a sign that the dividend may be cut.

Don't be entranced by a stock that sports an above-average yield without doing a lot of research. There must be a reason why the yield is that high, and it probably is not positive. Be suspicious of stocks with ultra-high yields relative to their peers.

Off the Beaten Path—Out-of-Favor Stocks. Since the way to make money in stocks is to buy low and sell high, buying stocks when they are out of favor could be a good way to buy low. Just as investors can inordinately bid up the price of a growth stock, they can also pummel a stock causing it to slip to unrealistically low prices. That's where bargain hunters swoop in; conversely, they attempt to sell when the stock has recovered.

One way to spot out-of-favor stocks is by looking for low P/E ratios relative to the company's peers. A P/E ratio of less than 10 may signal that investors do not have much hope for the company. If they are wrong, and the company reports better-than-expected results, perceptions can change quickly, and the stock price can shoot up. Do your research first. Some companies deserve their low valuation.

In addition to a low P/E ratio, bargain hunters usually look for industries that are currently out of favor. Other signs include (1) few of the shares are held by institutional investors, such as mutual funds and pension plans, and (2) few Wall Street analysts are following the stock. Look for a stock with a strong chance at turnaround. Signs that recovery is on the way may include one or more of the following: (1) a halt in the deterioration of sales and earnings, (2) a new product or service that has the potential to restart the company's growth, (3) company executives are buying the stock, (4) the company is "buying back," i.e., repurchasing their own shares, and (5) capital expenditures are increasing.

Bargain Hunter's Paradise—Value Stocks. If you could buy a stock worth $10 for $8, would you do it? Most people would because they know they are buying something for less than it is currently worth. In the stock market, this strategy is known as *value investing.*

The key to value investing is the ability to perceive when a stock's price does not fully reflect the value of the enterprise and its assets. Those assets might include real estate, plant and equipment, brand names, patents, or even cash or stocks in other companies. Value investors make money by buying when the stock's assets are worth more than the stock's price and selling when the value of the assets has been realized because (1) it has been purchased by another company; (2) it is broken into pieces, leaving shareholders with several stocks worth more separately than they were worth as a whole; (3) management figures out how to make the formerly underused asset more productive, producing higher profits; or (4) investors finally realize the value of the company's assets and buy the stock, causing its price to rise.

Trying to determine the true value of assets is tricky, but not as difficult as determining a fair price for the stock of a company. A valuable asset to one investor may have far less worth to another. Still, you can get a sense of whether a stock is selling for less than its breakup value by looking at the company's book value per share, tangible assets per share like land or oil reserves, and financial assets including cash and securities.

Hairpin Turns: New Issues. Probably one of the most exciting yet dangerous opportunities in the stock market is new issues, the initial public offerings (IPOs) of privately held companies. Such companies usually "go public" with great fanfare and hype, which can make their stock prices soar immediately after they begin trading.

The new issues market is extremely sensitive to the general direction of the stock market. When stock prices are high and rising and investors are enthusiastic, many privately held companies go public. When prices are low and depressed and no one wants to hear about stocks, it is almost impossible to sell a new issue.

IPOs usually occur when their industries are popular with investors. What's hot goes in and out of fashion quite frequently. In the late 1990s, high-tech Internet and communications companies were hot, but the bubble burst in 2001; although in 2004 Google, an Internet search engine, went public to much hoopla and in its first six months more than doubled its price.

By their nature, new issues are speculative because they usually have no history of performance as public corporations. Several studies have shown that in the long term, about a third of all new issues do well, a third don't move much from the price at which they go public, and a third go bankrupt. Another study found that IPOs jump an average of 15 percent on their first day of trading, and then underperform the market by 44 percent over the ensuing three years. Therefore, these stocks are not appropriate as college savings vehicles.

Highway 2: Bond Overview

When you invest in a bond, you are lending the issuer of that bond your money in return for a fixed rate of interest and a promise to repay the "loan" at a specific date in the future. Normally, you receive interest payments every six months, and when the bond matures, you receive your original principal, no matter how much the price of the bond fluctuated since you bought it.

Bonds are one of the key investment vehicles for achieving your financial goals. They allow you to lock in a set rate of income for a long period of time, which can give your financial plan a rock-solid foundation. Chances are that at some stage bonds or other fixed-income securities will play an important role in your financial plan. They can be a very appropriate vehicle for college funding.

Bonds are normally quoted on a price scale of 0 to 200, with 100 being the price at which the bond was issued, known as par. Because bonds are sold in denominations of $1,000, 100 means that the bond is trading at $1,000 per bond or 100 percent of the issue price. If the bond's price rises to 110, your holding is now worth $1,100.

Unlike stock transactions, bond buy-and-sell transactions normally occur without a separate commission charge. Instead, a broker makes money by taking a piece of the spread between the buying and selling prices. For example, if you buy a bond at a price of 100, the broker might charge you 102, keeping the two percentage points as a commission. If you sell a bond for a price of 100, you might get only 98. If you hold a bond until maturity there is no "sale" and therefore no additional cost.

This is very important because the bond market is generally dominated by large institutions that trade millions of dollars' worth of bonds; therefore brokers take a wider spread if you buy only a small number of bonds. Many bond brokers won't even execute a trade for fewer than 25 bonds, or $25,000, though some might go as low as five bonds, or $5,000, but you often pay a higher price to buy smaller quantities. Because it is a competitive market, you should shop around among brokers to get the best deal.

The only way you can avoid paying a large spread for small purchases, other than to buy bonds through a mutual fund, is to buy government bonds directly from the Treasury. You can buy bills, notes, and bonds whenever the Treasury auctions new issues. You can also buy U.S. savings bonds for only $25 through any bank or possibly by payroll deduction. (Government bonds are discussed in more detail in the next section.)

Side Trips: Categories of Bonds

Now that you understand the basics of bonds, it is time to discuss the advantages and disadvantages of the various types of bonds. Selecting the best bonds for you depends on the size of your assets, your financial goals, your time horizon, your risk tolerance, your tax situation, and your knowledge level. The following sections touch on each kind of bond, starting with the most conservative (Treasuries) and ending with the most speculative (junk bonds).

Smooth Sailing—Treasury Securities. Any Treasury security that is issued with a maturity of one year or less is called a Treasury bill or T-bill. They are usually auctioned to the public every Monday in three- and six-month maturities (called 13-week and 26-week bills). Normally, the longer you commit your money, the higher the yield.

You can buy a Treasury bill directly from any Federal Reserve Bank or branch by mail, with no fee or through the Treasury Direct program at http://www.TreasuryDirect.org. If you keep $100,000 or less in the program, there is no charge. If you keep $100,000 or more, the Treasury charges you an annual fee of $25. You must fill out a form and submit a check for at least $10,000, the minimum accepted for a Treasury bill purchase, and agree to accept whatever yield emerges from the Treasury auction at which you are bidding. Alternatively, you can buy a Treasury bill through any broker or bank for a charge of about $25, which, of course, reduces your effective yield. The supply of and demand for bills ultimately determine the average yield on each T-bill auction.

> *Whenever you investigate another bond's default risk, yield, after-tax return, and ease of trading, compare it to what a Treasury Security with a similar maturity offers.*

T-bills provide the ultimate in safety and liquidity and are, therefore, among investors' favorite havens for cash. Treasury bills are backed by the U.S. government, so for all practical purposes, they carry no risk of default. For this reason they are the benchmark against which all other bonds are compared.

Treasury notes work just like bills except that notes have shorter maturities. Treasury notes are issued in minimum denominations of $1,000 and also in $5,000, $10,000, $100,000, and $1 million sizes. To invest in Treasury notes, you put up your $1,000 (or more) and receive interest checks every six months. Under a program called Treasury Direct, you can purchase Treasury securities and have your interest checks deposited electronically in any bank or financial institution you choose.

If you need to cash in your T-bill before maturity, you can sell it but may not receive the best price. If interest rates have risen between the time you bought it and when you want to sell it, the T-bill's price will have dropped. Treasury bills might be right for you if you want total security from default (meaning that you can hold it until maturity, if necessary), marketability, and have a minimum of $10,000 to invest.

A big advantage of U.S. government bonds is that all the interest you earn is exempt from state and local taxes. By avoiding state and local taxes on Treasury securities, your effective after-tax yield is actually a bit higher than you might think, particularly if you live in a high-tax city or state like New York or California. For example, say you own a Treasury bond worth $10,000 that is yielding 5 percent, or $500, a year. If your combined city and state tax rate is 10 percent, you have avoided paying the $50 in city and state taxes that would otherwise have been due. But you are not exempt from federal income tax on your Treasury bond interest, you must pay that.

In return for the safety, marketability, and tax advantages, you receive a lower yield than is available from other bonds. How much lower depends on the current market conditions and the bonds to which you compare Treasuries. But for conservative income-oriented investors, Treasuries are definitely worth considering.

Treasury Inflation Protection Securities (TIPS). TIPS are a relatively new investment vehicle and not as widely traded as other Treasury issues. TIPS offer the investor a hedge against inflation, because their principal value is adjusted to reflect changes in the consumer price index (CPI). Interest is calculated using the adjusted principal amount and paid semiannually.

TIPS are available directly from the Treasury. They are auctioned, as ten-year notes, quarterly by the U.S. Treasury. TreasuryDirect (http://www.treasurydirect.gov) provides no-fee transactions and allows the direct debiting of your bank account. Bonds are available in denominations of $1,000 and multiples thereof. Investors can invest up to $5 million at one auction. TIPS also can be bought through a bank or broker; however, you probably will be required to maintain an account and pay commission.

TIPS are exempt from state and local income taxes but subject to federal income taxes. Interest and any gains when the principal grows are considered reportable income and taxable in that year. TIPS work best in tax-advantaged accounts that allow tax deferral.

If the inflation-adjusted principal amount at maturity is less than the principal amount at issuance, the original principal amount is paid. Even in a deflationary period, the original principal is guaranteed. Prices of TIPS will rise and fall with the rise and fall of interest rates, just like ordinary bonds (although probably not as much).

Snapshot—U.S. Savings Bonds. Like Treasuries, savings bonds have the backing of the U.S. government and the interest they pay is free from state and local taxes. Unlike Treasuries, though, savings bonds are available in much smaller denominations. You can buy a savings bond at any bank or possibly through your company by payroll deduction, for as little as $25 or as high as $10,000 apiece, up to a maximum of $15,000 a year.

Series EE savings bonds are issued at half their face value. When you buy a $50 bond, for example, you pay $25 for it. They have no set maturity date and pay no current interest, but you can redeem them any time—from within six months of buying them to as long as 30 years later, according to a redemption schedule published by the Treasury Department. Depending on when the bond was issued, it has a different original maturity date, which is the maximum amount of time it takes for the bond to reach face value.

Series EE savings bonds, though they do not offer any capital appreciation potential, can provide a solid base for funding at least part of your child's college education.

The yields on savings bonds issued on May 1, 1997 or later are based on 90 percent of the average yields of five-year Treasury securities for the preceding six months. These bonds increase in value every month and interest is compounded semiannually.

I-bonds are another type of U.S. savings bond and are designed for investors seeking to protect the purchasing power of their investment and earn a guaranteed real rate of return. I-bonds are an accrual-type security, meaning the interest is added to the bond monthly and paid when the bond is cashed. I-bonds are sold at face value—you pay $50 for a $50 bond—and grow in value with inflation indexed earnings for up to 30 years.

Series EE Savings Bonds and the Series I Inflation Protection Bonds are an especially good way to pay for college and save on taxes. Individuals can purchase up to $15,000 of Series EE bonds ($30,000 face value) and $30,000 (issued at face value) Series I bonds per year. The interest from these bonds is tax-exempt when used to pay for qualified educational expenses, if the required conditions are met. If you take the bond route, keep these things in mind:

1. Bonds must have been issued after December 31, 1989, to receive preferential tax treatment; purchaser must be over age 24 at the time of purchase; and bonds must be purchased in the parents' names. If bonds previously purchased are titled incorrectly, there is a procedure to get them retitled, provided that the parents initially purchased the bonds and the parents' income is below the eligibility limits at the time of redemption.

2. Redemption must be in the year of qualified expenses. In your records, include the bonds' serial number, face value, issue date, redemption date, total proceeds (principal and interest), receipt from the educational institution receiving the payment, and receipts for qualified expenses.

3. Interest on the bonds can be partially or completely tax-free, depending on the parents' income (indexed for inflation) in the year of redemption.

4. For tax purposes, bonds are considered a parental asset, and the interest is deemed paid income. The IRS adds redemption interest to your income before determining eligibility for the tax break, also affecting your adjusted gross income (AGI) for financial aid purposes.

5. Qualified expenses include tuition and fees but not room, board, and books.

6. Purchasing bonds in smaller denominations provides more flexibility, because any redemption amount that exceeds the amount of qualified expenses loses its tax-free treatment.

Savings bonds may appeal to families that expect to meet the income limitations at redemption, have a low risk tolerance and short time horizon, and are willing to accept the relatively low returns.

Savings bonds have a lot going for them. If you sign up to receive them as part of a payroll savings plan, you receive an added benefit: You build capital automatically, which will come in handy in accumulating money for college.

Broad Vista—Government Agency Securities. One notch riskier than Treasuries and U.S. savings bonds are the securities issued by a plethora of federal-government-backed agencies. Though they do not have the full faith and credit of the U.S. government behind them, you can be fairly certain the Congress would find a way to make sure these agencies didn't default on their debt. A default is very unlikely; yet, because agency securities are not thought to be as completely risk free as Treasury securities, their yields are slightly higher.

Like interest from Treasuries, interest from agency securities is usually taxable at the federal level but exempt from state and local taxes. The two major exceptions to this rule are mortgage-backed securities of the Federal National Mortgage Association (Fannie Mae) and the Government National Mortgage Association (Ginnie Mae). (The next section discusses mortgage-backed securities in more detail.) As with any bond, you must pay a capital gains tax if you sell a federal agency bond before maturity for a profit.

Unlike Treasuries, federal agency securities are not auctioned directly to the public, but are easy to buy through any traditional or discount brokerage firm. Depending on the agency, the bonds come in minimum denominations of $1,000 to $25,000.

Whether a federal agency bond is right for you depends on its current yield and whether you feel comfortable with the slightly greater risk involved in owning one.

Local Trip—Municipal Bonds. Though riskier than Treasury and possibly agency securities, municipal bonds (munis) are extremely popular. These bonds, issued by states, cities, counties, towns, villages, and taxing authorities of many types, have one feature that separates them from all other securities: The interest they pay is *totally free* from federal taxes, and, in most cases, bondholders who are also residents of the states issuing the bonds do not have to pay state taxes on the interest either. If you buy a bond issued by the city you live in you may avoid paying local tax on the interest paid on these bonds. Bonds not taxable by the resident state are known as double-tax-exempt bonds, and those also not taxable by a locality are called triple-tax-exempt issues. Keep these taxation rules in mind when you are deciding whether it makes more sense to buy an in-state bond or an out-of-state bond.

The fact that the interest from municipal bonds is federally tax free allows issuers to sell bonds with yields lower than taxable government and corporate bond issuers must pay. Some investors are better off financially to earn 6 percent tax free, rather than 8 percent on a Treasury, on which federal taxes are due. The higher your federal, state, and local tax bracket, the more attractive munis become.

To buy municipal bonds, you must go through a broker. Municipal bonds are usually issued in minimum denominations of $5,000, though some are issued in lots as small as $1,000.

When shopping for a municipal bond, ask if it is callable. If it is, ask how many years of protection against early redemption you will receive. Many municipal bond investors have been shocked in recent years when they received their principal back much sooner than they expected it.

General obligation and revenue bonds are the two main types of municipal bonds. General obligation bonds (GOs) are issued by a state or local entity and are backed by the taxing power of that state, city, or town. These tend to be the safest type of municipal bond. Revenue bonds finance specific revenue-producing projects, such as toll roads, bridges, tunnels, sewer systems, or airports, and the interest and principal paid by the bonds comes from the economic activity generated by the bonds. Some revenue bonds are riskier than others.

The best way to judge the safety of any particular issue is to look at the bond's safety rating by Standard & Poor's, Moody's, or Fitch. If you would rather not worry at all about safety, invest in insured mutual bonds. Insured bonds usually trade as though they have an AAA (excellent) rating because no risk of default exists. However, the cost of the insurance is passed on to the investor; insured bonds usually yield a little less than similar noninsured bonds.

Clearly, if you are in a high enough tax bracket, it pays to investigate municipal bonds. They are not only safe, their after-tax yields can often beat any other taxable fixed income alternatives.

Promontory—Corporate Bonds. The next rung down the ladder of bond risk are bonds issued by corporations.

Because corporations, no matter how solid financially, are perceived as vulnerable to changes in the business environment, the bonds they issue are considered riskier than government issues. Therefore, they generally pay a higher yield than government issues of the same maturity. Still, only a tiny percentage of corporate bonds—typically less than 1 percent—ever default.

Depending on the financial creditworthiness of the issuing company, a corporate bond can yield from 1 to 4 percentage points more than Treasuries of the same maturity.

As with all bonds, you can profit if you buy them when interest rates are high and hold them until maturity or sell them if rates fall and bond prices have climbed. Corporate bond prices react to general fluctuations in interest rates, as well as the financial fortunes (or misfortunes) of the issuing companies.

A Distant Shore—Foreign Bonds. You need not restrict your search for solid, income-producing bonds to U.S. securities. There's a big world beyond our shores, and it is filled with opportunities in highly rated, high-yielding bonds issued by foreign governments and foreign-based corporations.

Foreign government bonds, like U.S. Treasuries, are backed by the full faith and credit of the issuing countries. While that sounds comforting, the guarantee has more weight coming from an industrialized country like Germany or France than from a developing country like Kenya or Costa Rica. Because most investors do not want to worry about receiving their interest and principal, the foreign government bonds that trade most actively in the United States are issued by industrialized countries. Most U.S. brokers can sell foreign government bonds, though the easiest ones to trade are so-called "Yankee" bonds, which are issued in the United States by foreign governments and are denominated in dollars.

The bonds that are most actively traded are those issued by large, well-known foreign-based corporations.

Most foreign bonds—government and corporate—even Yankee bonds, come in minimum denominations much higher than those of domestic issues. Depending on the country, you might have to invest at least $25,000.

Foreign bonds might make sense for you for two reasons: (1) the yields on foreign bonds can be significantly higher than those on similar domestic issues, and (2) their value to U.S. investors can rise if the U.S. dollar falls against the foreign currencies (but that means it can fall as the dollar rises). So, in the best of all worlds, your foreign bond can give you not only a high yield but capital gains as well.

Foreign corporate bonds have drawbacks similar to foreign government bonds. Therefore, when you consider buying a foreign bond, evaluate whether the dollar seems to be getting stronger or weaker. It's best to wait until you think the dollar is getting weaker. Despite the potential high yields and profits from foreign bonds, most individuals play this market by buying mutual funds that specialize in foreign bonds (see the section on mutual funds).

Long and Winding Road—Zero-Coupon Bonds. These bonds—called zeros for short—can, paradoxically, be the safest of all investments or the riskiest. It all depends on how you use them. A zero-coupon bond gets its name from the fact that the bond is issued with a zero percent coupon rate. This means that instead of making regular interest payments, a zero is issued at a deep discount from its face value of 100, or $5,000. The return on a zero comes from the gradual increase in the bond's price from the discount to face value, which it reaches at maturity.

This slow but steady rise in value yields three benefits: (1) You know exactly how much money you will receive when the bond matures; (2) You know exactly when you will receive that money; and (3) You do not have to worry about reinvesting the small amounts of interest regular full-coupon bonds pay.

The other attraction of a zero is that your interest is reinvested automatically at the zero's yield. This can be a particularly significant advantage if you lock in a high interest rate. With a regular interest-paying bond, you receive interest checks every six months, which can be helpful if you need the money for current tuition payments.

Although there are many issuers of zero-coupon bonds, most investors buy zeros based on Treasury bonds, commonly known as *STRIPS*, which are backed by the U.S. government and are noncallable. Some brokerage firms have launched their own versions of STRIPS. Several large corporations issue zero-coupon bonds that allow you to lock in higher yields than do government issues, but are riskier (you do not want to wait 20 years with no payoff, only to discover that the issuing corporation went bankrupt).

Taxable zero-coupon bonds have one major pitfall. The Internal Revenue Service (IRS) has ruled that the scheduled yearly growth in the value of a zero-coupon bond (the IRS calls it the bond's accretion) must be considered interest income in the year it is earned, even though you do not receive any cash interest payments. The IRS publishes an accretion table, telling you how much "imputed" interest you must report each year. This rule can take much of the zip out of zeros because every year, you must pay taxes on interest without having received the interest to pay the taxes.

You have two ways to get around this dilemma: buying zeros only in tax-sheltered accounts or buying tax-free municipal zero-coupon bonds. If you buy a zero through an individual retirement account (IRA), a Keogh account, a salary reduction plan, or some other vehicle that allows you to defer tax liability until you withdraw money from the account, the IRS accretion rules do not affect you. The zero compounds year after year, untouched by taxes. You pay taxes on the increased value only when you withdraw the money, usually at retirement or to pay for your child's education.

You never owe taxes on the interest paid by municipal bonds, and the same holds true for muni zeros. You can therefore buy muni zeros in your taxable account and watch them compound tax free until they mature. The fact that muni zeros offer such superb benefits makes them extremely popular, which often means they sell out soon after they are issued. Therefore, if you think a muni zero is right for you, contact your broker before a new bond is issued so that they can grab a few bonds while they last. When shopping for muni zeros, look carefully at the call provisions of the issues because many allow issuers to redeem them before their scheduled maturity, which could defeat your whole purpose of buying them.

The risky side of zeros. So far, we have described zeros as the safest and surest way to fund a distant financial goal; however, there is another far more volatile side to zeros if you use them to earn capital gains. Because zeros lock in a fixed reinvestment rate of interest for a long time, their prices react to fluctuations in interest rates far more than any other type of bond. For every one-point drop in interest rates over a year, for example, a normal 30-year coupon bond paying 8 percent would produce a total return (price change plus income) of 20 percent, while a 30-year zero with an 8 percent reinvestment rate would soar by 42 percent. Conversely, if interest rates rose by one percentage point over a year, the full-coupon bond would suffer a negative total return of 3 percent, while the zero-coupon bond yielding 7 percent would plunge by 19 percent. The fact that the zero compounds its yield automatically for many years magnifies the impact of interest rate changes. The effect of interest rate changes on zeros is lessened if the zeros are of a shorter maturity.

If you want a diversified portfolio of zeros, you can buy shares in a zero-coupon bond mutual fund for a minimum of $1,000. The largest fund company offering zero-coupon funds is American Century Investments.

Put the Top Down—Convertible Bonds. Convertible bonds are hybrids; they have qualities of both bonds and stocks. In their role as bonds, they offer regular fixed income though usually at a yield lower than straight bonds of the same issuer. In their role as stocks, convertibles offer significant appreciation potential and a way to benefit from the issuing companies' financial success. However, owners of convertibles will not benefit as much as common stockholders if the companies' fortunes soar.

To some investors, convertibles offer the best of both worlds—high income and appreciation potential. To others, convertibles offer the worst of both worlds—lower income than bonds yield and less appreciation potential than common stock offers. Whichever way you view them, convertibles can make a solid contribution to your investment portfolio.

Convertible prices tend to fall less than stock prices when the stock market declines because convertibles offer a higher level of income than most stocks, which tends to cushion the convertibles' descent. Conversely, when the stock market surges convertibles tend to rise less than stocks do. Depending on the size of the convertible issue, the stature of the issuer, and the credit rating of the bond from the ratings agencies, trading may be very active or inactive.

Convertibles offer no special tax breaks. All interest paid is fully taxable at the federal, state, and local levels. Although no taxes are due if you convert from a bond to common stock, you must pay all the normal taxes on the stock dividends and capital gains taxes if you sell, before maturity, a convertible for a profit.

Hazard!

A Ride in the Country or Road to Nowhere?

Before you buy any convertible, decide whether you want to own the issuer's common stock. If you think the underlying company has a bright future, the convertible can be an excellent choice to improve your current income and profit from the firm's success. However, if you are considering the convertible only for the income, and you would not want to be caught holding the underlying stock, move on to another option. Despite all the bells and whistles of convertibles, they are ultimately just another way to invest in a company's prospects.

Curves Ahead—Junk Bonds. The riskiest type of bond is known in the brokerage industry as high-yield bonds, also called junk bonds. Junk bonds are issued by corporations that have less than an investment-grade rating. That means Standard & Poor's and Fitch rate them below BBB, and Moody's rates them below Baa. Companies earn such low ratings for two reasons: They are either up-and-comers (companies that do not have the long track record of sales and earnings) or fallen agents (corporations that attained an investment-grade rating in previous years by diligently increasing sales and profits, but for one reason or another things changed, causing the ratings agencies to downgrade the firms' bonds).

While a low safety rating might be bad news for a company, it can be good news for investors because it means that the firm's bonds will pay a substantially higher yield than will securities issued by more financially stable corporations. How much more depends on which issuers you compare, but decent-quality junk bonds often yield between 2 and 5 percentage points more than investment-grade issues. That can translate into yields of 8 to 12 percent.

The interest you receive from a junk bond is fully taxable at the federal, state, and local levels. If you sell (before maturity) the bond for a gain, you must pay capital gains tax. If the company defaults on its bonds and ultimately liquidates, all you can do is write off your losses against other capital gains and up to $3,000 of ordinary income.

Whether you invest in junk bonds depends on your ability to tolerate high risk in return for high yields and some potential for capital gains. However, don't put too much of your money into junk bonds. The risk is just not worth the angst.

A safer alternative than buying individual high-yield bonds is to buy a mutual fund that purchases a widely diversified portfolio of the high-yield issues. That way, you have a professional manager picking through the junk for you.

Highway 3: Mutual Fund Overview—Stocks

Put simply, a stock mutual fund is a pool of money that a fund manager invests in stocks to achieve a specific objective. The fund is sponsored by a mutual fund company, which may be an independent firm, such as Fidelity, T. Rowe Price, or Vanguard, or a division of a brokerage or insurance company, like Merrill Lynch, Smith Barney, or Kemper.

Load versus No-Load Funds. There are two basic kinds of mutual funds, differentiated by the method by which they are sold. One kind of fund is called a load mutual fund because you have to pay a commission to a salesperson to buy it; the other, called a no-load fund, is bought directly from the mutual fund company or a discount broker, with no salesperson involved.

Both load and no-load funds have their roles in the marketplace, and you must decide which is best for your needs. The advantage of a load fund is that you receive professional advice on which fund to choose. Such advice may be well worthwhile because it might be difficult for you to isolate the few funds that are best for your situation among the more than 18,000 funds in existence. Ideally, the salesperson helping you will not only tell you which types of funds to buy but also when to sell all or part of your shares and move your money to a better option.

Hazard!

Read the Fine Print

Some mutual funds levy additional charges, which you should know before you invest. They are all disclosed in a standardized fee table on the front of all fund prospectuses. Note that funds are required to detail their expenses by category for the last year, and must project what that would cost investors if they invested $1,000 over the next year, three, five, and 10 years so that you can compare similar funds.

The disadvantage of a load fund is that the commission reduces the amount of money you have at work in the fund. The load can be as high as 8.5 percent of your initial investment or as little as 3 percent or 4 percent. Thus, every dollar you invest is reduced by anywhere from 3 to 8½ cents. In the short term, therefore, you are starting at a disadvantage over a no-load fund, where all of your dollar is at work from the beginning.

Clearly, the advantage of the no-load fund is that you have all of your money working for you from the moment you open your account. The disadvantage of a no-load fund is that you will not receive much, if any, guidance on which fund to buy. When you call a no-load company's toll-free number, the representative can explain the differences among the firm's offerings, and can describe each fund's investment objective, track record, dividend yield, asset size, management style, fees, and the stocks currently in its portfolio, but they cannot advise you on which fund to buy. Some discount brokers work with no-load funds in the same way; others also provide some direction if the investor is looking for that. If you know what you want and prefer to take full responsibility for your investment decisions that may not be a problem. There are also independent fee-only financial advisors who charge by the hour and provide specific investment advice regarding no-load funds, as well as most other investment vehicles.

Both no-load and load funds levy what is known as a management fee every year to compensate them for the services they render. The management fee, which ranges from as little as .2 percent of your assets to as much as 2 percent, is deducted from the value of the fund automatically. So, if a fund charges a 1 percent management fee, for example, and the fund's stock portfolio rose 10 percent over the past year, you will earn a 9 percent return. The management fee, listed in a fund's selling literature as part of the expense ratio, should not be much more than 1.25 percent of its (and therefore your) assets for it to be considered fair and reasonable.

Side Trip: Choosing the Best Stock Fund for You

As with all investments, before you invest in any fund, you should review your financial goals, your time horizon, your risk tolerance level, and your investment philosophy. Also, you should place each fund you consider at its appropriate level in the investment pyramid.

The following is a rundown of the different categories of stock funds, separated into the sectors of the investment pyramid.

High-Risk Funds

Aggressive growth funds. These funds buy stocks of fast-growing companies or of other companies that have great capital gains potential. They might also buy stocks in bankrupt or depressed companies, anticipating a rebound. Such funds often trade stocks frequently in hope of catching small price gains.

Foreign stock funds. These funds buy stocks of corporations based outside of the United States. In addition to the usual forces affecting stock prices, fluctuations in the value of the U.S. dollar against foreign currencies can dramatically affect the price of these funds' shares, particularly over the short term.

Sector funds. Sector funds buy stocks in just one industry or sector of the economy; for example, technology stocks, utilities, and natural resources. Because these funds are not diversified outside of their sector, they soar or plummet on the fate of the industry in which they invest.

Hazard!
Avoid the Dollar Cost Averaging Toll Trap

Each time you buy a front load mutual fund you incur commission charges, which greatly reduce your gains. To avoid this problem, you can execute dollar cost averaging using a no-load mutual fund.

Small-company growth funds. Such growth funds invest in stocks of small companies, typically those having outstanding shares with a total market value of $1 billion or less. These companies may have enormous growth potential, yet the stocks they invest in are much less established—and therefore riskier—than large companies in mature industries.

Moderate-Risk Sector Funds

Growth funds. Growth funds invest in shares of well-known growth companies that usually have a long history of increasing earnings. Because the stock market fluctuates, growth funds rise and fall as well, just not as much as funds holding smaller, less proven stocks.

Equity-income funds. Such funds own shares in stocks that pay higher dividends than growth funds do. Whereas a growth fund's payout may be zero percent to 1 percent, an equity-income fund might yield 2 percent or 3 percent. That higher yield tends to cushion the fund's price when stock prices fall. When stock prices rise, equity-income funds tend to increase less sharply than do pure growth funds.

A slightly more aggressive version of an equity-income fund is called a growth and income fund or a total return fund because it strives for gains from both income and capital appreciation.

Index funds. These funds buy the stocks that make up a particular index to allow investors' returns to match the index. The most popular of these use the Standard & Poor's 500 as their benchmark. Proponents of index funds argue that because many money managers fail to match or beat the S&P 500 each year, investors can come out ahead by just matching the index. Because there is no research or decision-making involved, the management fees of an index fund are much lower than those of other stock funds.

Low-Risk Sector Funds

Balanced funds. Balanced funds keep a fairly steady mix of high-dividend, large company stocks and quality bonds. This allows the funds to pay a fairly high rate of current income and still participate in the long-term growth of stocks.

Asset allocation funds. These funds have the latitude to invest in stock, bonds, or cash instruments, depending on the fund manager's market outlook. If the manager thinks stock prices are about to fall, some or all of the assets can be shifted into cash instruments to avoid losses. If they think stock prices are about to rise funds can be moved into stocks. Usually, the fund will always have some money in stocks, bonds, and cash, which tends to stabilize its performance.

Utilities funds. Such funds buy shares in electric, gas, telephone, and water utilities, which have steady earnings and pay high dividends. Utilities funds are subject to swings in interest rates, however. Nonetheless, for a high-yielding and relatively stable stock fund, a utilities fund is worth considering.

Once you have chosen the fund categories that fit your needs, you must narrow your options further by looking at the best funds within each category (we'll be traveling this road in Chapter 4).

A Brief Detour: Closed-End Mutual Funds

So far, we've been discussing open-end funds. Another variety of fund is called a closed-end fund, which has its own advantages and disadvantages. Like open-end funds, closed-end funds offer professional management, diversification, convenience, and automatic reinvestment of dividends and capital gains.

The difference is in the way you buy shares. Open-end funds create new shares continually, as more money is invested in them. When cash is taken out of the fund, the number of outstanding shares shrinks. The portfolio manager therefore is faced with an ever-changing pool of assets that can be small one month and huge the next. This can make it difficult to manage the fund because millions of dollars usually pour into the fund after it has had a hot record and stock prices are high, and millions leave the fund when it has underperformed the market and stock prices are falling. This pattern of volatile cash flow can severely harm the fund's performance because, if the fund manager stays fully invested, the manager must buy stocks when prices are high and sell them when prices are low.

Closed-end funds are designed to avoid this problem. Instead of constantly creating and redeeming shares, these funds issue a limited number of shares, which trade on the New York or American Stock Exchanges or on the Nasdaq National Market System. Instead of dealing with the fund company directly when you buy or sell shares, you trade closed-end shares with other investors, just as you do any publicly traded stock. You pay traditional or discount brokerage commissions to buy and sell them, and you can look up the fund's price in the stock tables of the newspaper or on the Internet every day.

From the closed-end fund manager's point of view, there is no need to worry about huge flows of cash into and out of the fund. The manager knows how much money must be invested and selects stocks based on the fund's investment objective. This allows the manager to concentrate on meeting long-term objectives without worrying about keeping a stash of cash around to meet redemptions.

Like an open-end fund, a closed-end fund always has a certain net asset value (NAV, the worth of all the stocks in its portfolio divided by the number of shares). Unlike an open-end fund, a closed-ender can sell for more or less than the value of its portfolio, depending on demand for the shares and the underlying value of the stock with the portfolio. When the fund sells for more than its portfolio is currently worth, it is called selling at a premium. This usually happens when the fund is extremely popular and it offers some unique style or investing niche, which makes investors willing to pay a high price for it.

In general, closed-end funds tend to jump to premiums immediately after they first issue shares to the public because the brokerage firms that underwrite the issues actively promote them for a few months. Often, once the brokers have moved on to the next closed-end issue, the older funds drop to a discount. The moral of the story: It almost never pays to buy a new issue of a closed-end fund.

On the other hand, a fund investing in an unpopular category of stocks can fall to a steep discount. Closed-end funds can also drop to discounts because few people pay attention to them and, therefore, there is little demand for them. That can provide an opportunity to buy assets cheaply. In fact, if a fund's discount remains too deep for too long a time, raiders will often swoop in. Their game is to buy millions of shares at a discount, then force a vote to convert the fund from closed-end to open-end status. Because open-end funds always trade at the worth of their underlying portfolios, the raiders can walk off with huge profits.

Therefore, you should assess two factors when you buy a closed-end fund: (1) the fund manager's record in choosing winning stocks that allow the fund to achieve its investment objective, and (2) whether you are buying the fund at a premium or a discount. Some investors' entire strategy with closed-end funds is to buy them at a discount and wait for them to rise to a premium, at which point they sell.

To determine whether a fund is selling at a premium or a discount, you can look in Monday's *The Wall Street Journal* in the "Money and Investing" section or in *Barron's*.

There are several kinds of closed-end funds, each with its own objective and risk characteristics. Some of the most common types follow.

Bond funds. These funds buy either taxable government or corporate bonds or tax-free municipal bonds and pass the income on to shareholders.

Diversified equity funds. These funds buy a portfolio of stocks in many industries. If the fund manager is bearish (the manager thinks that the stock prices are over valued), though, the fund can hold cash or some bonds. The objective of diversified equity funds is usually growth.

International funds. International funds buy stocks in countries around the world. Their prices are therefore affected not only by changes in stock prices but also by fluctuations of foreign currencies against the U.S. dollar. Some international funds specialize in a particular area of the world, like Europe or Asia. Some specialize in stocks of developing countries. Some funds buy stocks in a particular industry, like health care or telecommunications, on a worldwide basis.

Sector and specialty funds. These funds specialize in the stocks of a particular industry such as banking, media, natural resources, or health care. Such funds have more potential for gain if the industry you pick does well but also have a higher risk of loss if the industry falls out of favor.

Single-country funds. Such funds invest in the stocks of a single country. This makes them more volatile than broadly diversified international funds.

Exchange Traded Funds (ETFs). These are one of the newer investment products and are similar to conventional mutual funds in that they provide investors an easy and affordable way to invest in a diversified group of securities. But, while mutual funds only can be bought or sold at the price at the end of each trading day, ETFs can be traded throughout the day, bought on margin, or sold short. Short selling and/or buying on margin may not be allowed in some accounts, specifically IRA accounts. In addition, only experienced investors with a stomach for risk should leverage their portfolios to buy investments on margin.

Among the most popular, best-known ETFs are

- ▶ Spiders (SPDR). A fund that tracks the S&P 500 Index.
- ▶ Diamonds (DIA). A pooled investment designed to provide results corresponding to price and yield performance, before fees and expenses, of the Dow Jones Industrial Average.
- ▶ Qubes (QQQ). A pooled investment designed to provide investment results that mirror the price and yield performance of the Nasdaq–100 Index.
- ▶ iShares. Like the Nasdaq Biotechnology Index Fund (IBB), which tracks the Nasdaq Biotechnology Index throughout the trading day, these follow a specialized index.
- ▶ Boulders (BLDRS). Baskets of listed depository receipts sponsored by and listed on the Nasdaq.

ETFs are attractive in that they can provide either broad or focused market exposure. They have low management fees and are tax-efficient investment vehicles. Capital gains-type transactions are minimized because ETFs do not have to issue or redeem stocks when individual investors place buy or sell orders, and because they are designed to track a static benchmark, they have fewer trades and lower turnover in their portfolios. But ETFs also carry buy/sell commissions that can add up over time, especially if the funds are bought or sold frequently, and negate their low-cost benefits.

Highway 4: Mutual Fund Overview—Bonds

If the process of choosing individual bonds seems too complicated, bond mutual funds might be right for you. Mutual funds offer several advantages to bond investors. The number one reason to buy a bond fund is for the simplicity of diversification.

For the most part, the bond market is designed for large institutional players who buy blocks of bonds, millions of dollars at a time, rather than small investors who buy a few thousand dollars' worth of securities. Bonds can be difficult to trade in small lots, so funds offer much better liquidity than do individual bonds, and you can buy or sell a mutual fund at that day's net asset value (NAV) and not have to worry about taking a bad price on a solo bond. By having a professional mutual fund manager on your side, you also pay much less in commission costs than you would as an individual investor buying the same bonds. Also, it is difficult to obtain good research on some bond types, particularly municipal, convertible, and junk bonds, and professionals will always have access to more detailed and timely information than you could get on your own.

Bond mutual funds offer other advantages. If you are an income-oriented investor, a bond fund portfolio can send you a monthly dividend check that will smooth out your cash flow. Individual bonds usually pay every six months, so you may receive a large amount of interest and then have to wait several months before the next payment. If you do not need the cash, bond funds offer automatic dividend reinvestment, which makes it far easier to buy more bonds than waiting for interest to accumulate until you meet the minimum for individual bonds. Finally, a bond fund is made up of tens, if not hundreds, of bonds, diversified by maturity, issuer, and quality. By spreading the risk around, you considerably soften the impact of a negative development on any particular bond. You could not afford such a diversified portfolio on your own, and you are exposed to serious loss if a problem develops with an individual bond.

One disadvantage of bond funds compared to individual bonds is that bond funds (except for zero-coupon bond funds) never mature. Bonds within a portfolio might mature, but the fund is constantly reinvesting the proceeds of matured or sold bonds back into more bonds. This means you have no guarantee that a bond fund will ever return to the price you purchased it at originally. For example, if you buy a fund when interest rates are low and then they rise a great deal, you might have to wait a long time for your principal value to return to where you started. With individual bonds, you can count on a fixed maturity date at which you will receive your original principal. The bond's price will bounce around while it is outstanding, but you can be assured that, in the end, you will get your money back—as long as the issuer does not default.

As with all individual bond prices, bond fund prices move inversely to interest rates. If rates rise, bond fund shares decline in price. As rates fall, bond fund prices rise. If you sell bond fund shares for more than you paid for them, you must pay capital gains tax on the difference. The income you

Roadmap 3.2

Bond Basics

Regardless of the type of bond or fixed income instrument you purchase, they tend to have certain common features:

1. Corporate and government bonds trade in $1,000 increments.
2. Municipal bonds trade in $5,000 increments.
3. Bonds have a "face value" or "par value" or "maturity value," which is what the bonds are expected to be worth when they mature.
4. They have a stated maturity date ranging from a few days to 30 to 40 years.
5. They have a stated interest rate, which is the percentage they are expected to pay based on the face value of the bond.
6. They may be rated by one of the rating services; Standard and Poor's and Moody's are two of the major ones. These services assign a letter rating based on the following scale:

	S&P	Moody's*
Highest Quality	AAA	Aaa
	AA	Aa
	A	A
	BBB	Baa
	BB	Ba
Low Quality	B	B

*The ratings continue but AAA through BBB are considered "investment grade bonds" with AAA being the highest quality and moving on to higher-risk and higher-yield bonds.

receive from a bond fund is taxable if the fund buys taxable bonds, and it is tax free if the fund invests in municipal securities.

As with other kinds of mutual funds, you can choose between no-load bond funds you buy directly from a fund company or discount broker, or load funds you buy through a commissioned broker or financial planner. As you shop around among bond funds, compare not only the yields but also the effect fees and expense levels will have on your return over time.

Side Trip: Categories of Bond Funds

Over the past several years, the number and variety of bond funds have mushroomed, as billions of dollars pour into bond funds each year. Thousands of funds now compete for your attention and bond fund companies continue to introduce new features already tested on other types of funds.

There are two factors that distinguish funds: (1) the kinds of securities they buy and (2) the average maturity of the bonds in their portfolios. In general, the longer it is until the fund's portfolio matures, the higher its yield, and the higher its risk. The following list describes different kinds of bond funds in terms of these two factors.

They have been separated according to the levels of the investment pyramid, from the most conservative to the most aggressive. As with any investment, you should review your financial goals, your time horizon, your risk tolerance level, and investment philosophy:

Low-Risk Sector

Government bond funds. Government bond funds invest exclusively in securities issued by the U.S. government or its agencies. No risk of default exists in any of the underlying securities; therefore, these are the safest bonds around. Long-term bond funds do carry substantial risk due to interest rate volatility, however.

Municipal bond funds. These funds invest solely in tax-exempt bonds, so all the dividends they pay are not subject to federal income tax. Depending on your tax bracket, these funds might allow you to keep more interest than you could earn on a higher yielding but taxable bond fund. Three kinds of muni bond funds are available:

1. National funds buy bonds from municipalities across the country. Interest from a state's bonds is taxable to out-of-state residents, so national bond funds will tell shareholders at the end of the year what percentage of the income they received came from such a state.
2. State-specific funds are designed by states for residents of those states who want to avoid both federal and state taxation. High-tax states, such as New York, California, Pennsylvania, and Michigan, offer many single-state funds because so much demand for them exists.
3. Local muni funds buy bonds only from a locality that levies an income tax, such as New York City. These bonds are therefore triple-tax-exempt

because they allow residents to sidestep federal, state, and local income taxes.

Municipal bond funds also are sold with portfolios composed totally of insured bonds. This insurance protects investors against the possibility of default by any issue a fund holds.

While state and local bond funds offer beneficial tax shelters, they are riskier than national funds because they are not diversified geographically. If a particular state or locality suffers a sharp downturn in its economy, all the bonds in the portfolio will probably be affected, which could cause shareholders in funds holding those bonds to suffer losses. Still, municipal bond funds, as a whole, are extremely safe; very few defaults have occurred.

Short- and intermediate-term bond funds. Such funds, which come in both taxable and tax-free varieties, buy bonds with maturities no longer than 10 years, and usually as short as two years. Because short-term bonds fluctuate in price far less than long-term bonds during the same interest rate volatility, these funds' prices remain quite stable. Many short-term funds offer check-writing privileges; therefore, many people use them as higher yielding alternatives to money-market funds. In cases where there is a significant difference between money-market rates and yields on short-term bond funds yields can be 1 or 3 percentage points higher than money funds. Unlike money funds, however, these funds' net asset values fluctuate and will fall if interest rates rise.

Moderate-Risk Sector

Convertible bond funds. Convertible bond funds buy convertible debentures and convertible preferred stocks. Though convertible yields are lower than those on straight corporate bonds, convertible bond funds offer more appreciation potential. These funds will provide their highest returns when the stock market is rising. The convertible market can be particularly confusing, and a good fund manager's expertise can be well worth the management fee.

High-grade corporate bond funds. Such funds buy bonds issued by investment grade corporations. The funds will pay yields of one or two percentage points higher than will government funds of similar maturities. Yet they remain quite safe because they buy top-quality bonds and diversify widely among hundreds of issues.

Mortgage-backed securities funds. These funds invest in mortgage-backed securities issued by quasi-governmental agencies, such as Ginnie Mae, Fannie Mae, and Freddie Mac. The securities they buy are guaranteed against default by those agencies but not against price fluctuations caused by interest rate movements. The other uncertainty that plagues mortgage-backed securities—the early prepayment of mortgage principal by homeowners—is taken care of by the fund manager, who automatically reinvests principal payments back into more securities.

This is a big advantage over holding individual Ginnie Maes or Freddie Macs because it is often difficult to reinvest the small amount of principal paid each month. Mortgage-backed securities funds tend to pay yields of one to 2 percentage points higher than similar maturity Treasury funds. Some mortgage-backed funds even permit check writing.

High-Risk Sector

Global bond funds. Global bond funds purchase bonds issued by governments and corporations from around the world. When interest rates are higher in countries other than the United States, these funds can pay yields significantly higher than similar domestic funds. Some funds try to use complicated futures and options strategies to hedge against currency swings, but the hedges do not always work, and they can be expensive, cutting the funds' yields.

The bonds these funds purchase are typically from top-rated governments and corporations, so there is little, if any, default risk. Global bond funds also come in short-term and long-term varieties. Short-term funds are less sensitive to currency swings, while long-term funds react more sharply both to interest rate movements and to changes in currency values.

High-yield junk bond funds. Junk bond funds buy bonds of corporations that are financially weaker than top-rated blue chip corporations; therefore, the bonds pay higher yields to compensate investors for the increased risk of default. Junk bond funds can pay yields four to six percentage points higher than government or high-grade corporate bond funds of similar maturities. High-yield fund prices are much more volatile than more conservative bond funds because of rapidly changing values of the bonds they hold. In general, junk bond funds perform well when the stock market rises because junk bonds mirror the performance of their issuers' stocks.

Zero-coupon bond funds. Such funds buy portfolios of zero-coupon bonds, and should be considered very conservative if they are held until they liquidate, which occurs when the bonds mature. However, because zero-coupon bonds are the most interest-rate sensitive of all bonds with the same maturity, these funds fluctuate more dramatically. Zero-coupon bond funds, which pay no dividends, soar in price when interest rates fall and plunge in price when interest rates rise.

A Brief Detour: Closed-End Bond Funds

All of the funds described above are open-end funds, which means they continually offer new shares to the public as new money flows into the funds. You should also consider shares in closed-end bond funds, which issue a limited number of shares and trade on the NYSE, AMEX, and the Nasdaq NMS.

Closed-end bond funds, like all closed-end stock funds, sell at either a premium or a discount to the current value of their bond portfolios. They typically sell at a premium to, or for more than, the portfolios' value when interest rates decline and investors scramble into closed-end bond funds in search of higher yields. But when interest rates rise, fund prices tend to shrink to a discount.

To calculate your effective yield, divide the annual dividend by the current price of the fund or look up these payouts in financial newspapers like *The Wall Street Journal* (on Mondays) and *Barron's*. They will list each bond fund's current price, NAV, and effective yield. You can also find the price and yield in NYSE, AMEX, and Nasdaq NMS tables because closed-end funds trade through these systems; or on the Internet, try http://finance.yahoo.com.

Closed-end bond funds, like their open-end cousins, come in both general and specialized categories. General funds can invest in any kind of bond that the fund's manager thinks will produce capital gains and income. These funds might have a combination of government, municipal, corporate, foreign, convertible, junk, and zero-coupon bonds as well as mortgage-backed securities in their portfolios. Their wide diversification makes them less risky than specialized funds, which buy only one type of bond. Still, a specialized fund might yield higher income if it invests only in tax-free municipal bonds or in high-yielding junk bonds, for example.

▶ Traveling On

Now that you've now gotten your feet wet, and familiarized yourself with the primary types of investments available to you, it's time to start considering which ones you should invest in. It is also time to decide whether you want to go it alone or take anyone along with you. So, let's move on to the next chapter and consider the pros and cons of advisors and where to park your college cash.

Flying Solo or Co-Piloting

What You Need to Know
Before You Go

Now that you have an understanding of the various types of investments available to you, there's another very important decision you should make before you leave home and begin investing your hard-earned money toward that goal. That is, do you want to do all this by yourself or do you want to share the driving with someone else? After all, in addition to saving for educating your kids, you will probably want to sock something away toward your retirement, possibly a new home or vacation retreat, and for life's other necessities and possibilities—large and small. Investing for all of these things can be time-consuming and the waters can be choppy. So consider this decision carefully.

In the first part of this chapter, we'll take a look at working with an advisor and offer some advice to those of you who decide to drive yourself to your destination. Don't forget, it's not an all or nothing decision; you can decide to use an advisor for parts of the trip, while you do some of the work yourself.

▶ Self-Guided Tour vs. Hiring a Guide: Making Investment Decisions

An advisor may be seen as an unnecessary expense or as an invaluable tool for your financial success. Some investors think the Internet has made the need for a qualified financial advisor unnecessary. For others, the sheer volume of material available on the Internet punctuates the need for advice.

> *The Internet is available 24 hours a day to provide information, but it cannot provide wisdom and experience.*

"I'm doing just fine on my own." Many people manage their own stock and/or mutual fund portfolios and get good returns. Some of these people are truly savvy investors, and others are fortunate beneficiaries of a great bull market and good timing. The more your portfolio grows, the more you may feel the need to get some help in managing your personal wealth. Many people seem quite content to remain alone while growing their assets, but that mindset is subject to change when the issue shifts to protecting those assets.

Ask yourself these two questions:

1. Do I know everything I need to know about asset allocation and protection, tax-reduction strategies, and how to provide the income I need when I need it?
2. Do I want to invest the time and effort to learn these issues? Do I want to continue to invest the time it takes to keep up with the markets and remain competent as an investor?

If you answered yes to these questions and have the time and interest in devoting yourself to building and protecting your assets, then you can go it alone.

If you know exactly what you want to own (stocks, bonds, mutual funds, etc.) and what allocation mix is appropriate for your goals, and know how to go about buying them at the best price, then you are the kind who can do it on your own. This assumes that you are well informed and can keep up on those holdings for any changes that could threaten the security of your investments.

> *Don't assume you know all there is to know. Even if you do it on your own, it may be wise to pay for a consultation in order to get some direction from a professional financial advisor. Some professionals consult for an hourly or for a one-time fee.*

You can also go it alone if you need only one financial service, like tax return preparation or auto insurance, and know where and how to go about securing those products or services. In such cases, it is probably not cost effective to hire a comprehensive financial planner. On the other hand, if you need an overall strategy that ties together the several aspects of your complex financial picture—past, present, and future—a planner's services may be invaluable.

Before you make a decision about which way to go, assess your situation to determine your long-term needs. For example, if you have specific long-term goals, such as funding your children's college education, a financial planner can start you on the right path.

How to Select a "Wealth-Building" Traveling Companion: Choosing a Financial Advisor

In the best of all worlds, the financial planner you hire would be a jack-of-all-financial-trades. Your planner would know everything about budgeting, investments, taxes, insurance, credit, real estate, employee benefits, estate planning, retirement, college financing, career advancement, and every other aspect of your financial life. The planner would help you assess where you stand now, what you want to accomplish, and how you can attain your goals. The planner would be personable and a good listener, would maintain objectivity, and would take on a role of fiduciary.

What to Look for. Do such paragons of virtue exist? Indeed they do, but to find one, you must weed out the incompetent and self-serving neophytes from the professionals who can help you obtain your financial goals.

Always remember one fact of economic life— you get what you pay for. If you refuse to pay a 5 percent load for a mutual fund that has produced 30 percent in returns the last five years, are you better off with a no-load fund that has returned 10 percent in the last five years? Of course not! In some cases you do get what you pay for.

The questions we need answered are simple: Is the service, expertise, and quality of the advice worth the fee you are paying? Is it giving you peace of mind? What are you willing to pay for that?

"I don't have enough money to talk to a professional." Many people have the idea that if they don't have $100,000, no professional will talk to them. Although most independent veteran advisors have minimum amounts they will work with, the majority of financial services salespeople and those advisors who don't sell products but rather advice on a fee-only, hourly basis will help individuals start their wealth-building process with whatever they have. You have to start somewhere, and your money is not going to grow by worrying that it's not enough. Don't let embarrassment convince you that your worth as an individual is measured by your fiscal net worth. Work with someone who will respect where you are—and build from there.

To begin, you need to establish a clear profile of the type of person you want to work with and start interviewing until you find a match that feels right to you. Finding a match is as much about personal chemistry as it is financial philosophy. The bottom line is that we need someone worthy of our trust.

What to Ask. As with any financial professional you consider hiring, arrange a face-to-face interview, where you can get a sense of the planner's personality and areas of expertise. Following are a few sample questions you should ask prospective financial advisors:

1. What services do you provide? Most planners will help you assemble a comprehensive plan, while others specialize in particular areas of finance. The services you should expect include cash management and budgeting; education funding; estate planning; investment review and planning; life, health, and property/casualty insurance review; retirement planning; goal and objective setting; and tax planning. Ask about each service you need specifically; for example, are you willing to assist with a very focused topic, such as college funding?

2. Will you show me a sample financial plan you have done? Without revealing confidential information or client names, the planner should be glad to show you the kind of plan you can expect when the data-gathering and planning process is complete.

3. What type of clientele do you serve? Some planners specialize by income category, age, or professional group. If you are nearing retirement, do not

hire a planner whose clients are mostly young entrepreneurs. If you are a dentist, you might look for a planning firm that specializes in serving dentists or other medical professionals.

4. Who will I deal with on a day-to-day basis? In larger planning firms, you might see the chief planner only at the beginning and end of the planning process and work with their associates in the meantime. If that is the case, meet the staff with whom you will be working, and ask about their qualifications.

5. Do you have access to other professionals if our planning process takes us into areas in which you are not an expert? A good planner has a network of top accountants, lawyers, insurance specialists, and investment pros to fall back on if they have questions.

6. Do you just give financial advice, or do you also implement the advice on a fee-only basis or by selling financial products? The great fault line in the financial planning industry lies between these two types of professionals.

7. Will your advice include specific product recommendations, or will you suggest only generic product categories? Most planners will name particular stocks or mutual funds, for example. Others will advise that you keep 50 percent of your assets in stocks, 30 percent in bonds, and 20 percent in cash, leaving you to determine which stocks, bonds, and cash instruments are appropriate.

8. Will you spend the time to explain your rationale for recommending a specific product and how it suits my goals, my tolerance for risk, and my circumstances? How do you plan to monitor a recommended mutual fund or investment product once I've bought it? You should feel comfortable that the planner will make the effort to ensure that you understand the strategy and products they recommend, and what their long-term service and advice policy is.

9. How will you follow up after you've delivered the plan to ensure that it is implemented? A good planner makes sure that you don't just file away the comprehensive plan and never put it into action. Not only should the plan be implemented, it also should be reviewed and revised as conditions in your life, tax laws, or the investment environment shifts.

10. How do you get compensated? Some planners charge for the advice they give. Others collect commissions from the sale of products they recommend. And still others charge both a planning fee and a sales charge.

(These styles are discussed further below.) However your planner gets paid, make sure that you receive a written estimate in advance of the advisor's total compensation from all sources and the amount you will be paying directly.

11. Are there any potential conflicts of interest in the investments you recommend? A planner must inform you, for example, if they or the firm earn fees as a general partner in a limited partnership that the planner touts and they must let you know that they receive commissions if they do. Unfortunately the advisor is not required to disclose how much compensation they receive. However, savvy consumers will ask for the specifics. They must also tell you if the planner receives some form of payment (commonly known as a referral fee) when they refer you to another firm, such as a law or an accounting firm.

12. Will you have direct access to my money? Some planners want discretionary control of their clients' funds, which allows the planners to invest as they see fit. Be extremely careful about agreeing to this arrangement, which is fraught with potential for fraud and malfeasance. If you do agree to it, make sure that the planner is bonded. This insurance will cover you in case the planner runs off with your money. Also, make certain that a reputable third-party custodian holds your assets and that you review your statements from this custodian regularly.

13. What professional licenses and designations have you earned? Besides looking on their walls for diplomas, inquire whether the planner holds a CFA, CFP, ChFC, CPA, or a PFS. Determine whether the planner is licensed to sell securities, which include stocks, bonds, partnerships, and mutual funds. If the planner wants to sell disability, life, and property/casualty insurance, as well as fixed or variable annuities, they need a license to sell insurance products. Also find out their educational background. If they started out as a lawyer, an insurance agent, an accountant, or some other specialist, it will most likely affect the advice the planner gives.

14. Is the planner registered as an investment advisor with the Securities and Exchange Commission or your state? All planners who provide investment advice should be registered with either the SEC or your state. If registered, the planner is required to give you Part II of Form ADV or a brochure containing the same disclosure information.

15. Have you ever been cited by a professional or governmental organization for disciplinary reasons? Even if the planner says that there has been no such trouble, you can check with the state attorney general's office, the state securities office, and the organizations that grant the professional designations held by the advisor. (See the "Resources" section at the end of this chapter for more information on these offices.)

How to Assess

Once you've met and interviewed the planner, the following assessment tool will greatly increase your odds of finding the wealth-building partner you need.

1. What was your first impression of the individual? Was the planner personable and respectful, or officious and/or arrogant? The individual's personality is a good indicator of the kind of service and attention you can expect to receive down the road should problems or concerns arise.

2. What kind of questions did the financial professional ask you? Were the questions more about your money or more about your life, values, and goals? The best people in the business know that they need to have clear understanding of where you've been, who you are, and where you want to go. Those who only inquire about your assets are only interested in your assets.

3. Did the financial professional demonstrate good listening skills? Did the individual carefully summarize your concerns, goals, and level of risk tolerance? If you get the feeling you are not dealing with a good listener, move on. If the individual is paying close attention now, you know that is what you can expect later. If the individual pretends to listen but just charges ahead with an agenda that seems to miss the point of what you said, move on. If the professional dominates the conversation, get out as fast as you can!

4. Did the financial professional explain matters in a language you could understand or was there too much jargon and the talk went over your head? Those who talk over your head probably want to keep you in the dark or simply aren't smart enough to make matters understandable. Anyone who makes you feel stupid is not worthy of your business. A sure sign of competence is the ability to make complex matters seem

simple and understandable. A good advisor will also be a good teacher and will help you improve your financial well-being.

5. Is the financial professional willing to disclose their personal holdings? You would be amazed at the number of financial professionals whose personal financial lives are a mess. There are also many who are not buying what they are recommending. If financial professionals are trying to sell something they don't own, you might want to know why. If you find an advisor who does for the clients what they do for themselves, you have a greater potential for trust.

6. Does the financial professional articulate a clear philosophy regarding investments and wealth building? If the professional doesn't have a clear philosophical compass that has been fine-tuned through experience, they are more likely to be one of those people who just follow the crowd. The dime-a-dozen advisor who sells whatever they are asked to sell is not the person you are looking for. I like to see advisors who are comfortable talking about their mistakes as well as their victories—a good investment philosophy borrows from the lessons of both failure and success.

7. Ask the financial professional what brought them into this business. You will hear answers ranging from seemingly being on a mission to help other people to those only pretending to be on a mission to help other people, while really thinking only of themselves. Read between the lines on this answer. You want to get the sense that the financial professional is fascinated about money matters, curious about people, and motivated to help you.

If you walk out of an interview satisfied that these bases have been covered, you have a great chance of partnering with a trustworthy individual. Cunning individuals may have the ability to fake these integral characteristics but they cannot fake them for long. You want a concerned and competent professional who is in the profession and wants to work with you for the right reasons. You want to find out what the person's motives are. After taking them through the preceding questions, you will have a pretty good indication.

What Services to Expect. Every financial advisor brings their own skills, talents, services, and, sometimes, products, to the table. You'll want to know what you can expect. Professional financial advisors provide advice and implementation assistance in the following areas:

Goal setting

Tax planning

Managing credit

Employee benefits

Business secession planning

Charitable gifting

Laddered maturity programs

Fixed/Variable annuities

Money management

Tax-free investing

Equity research

Over-the-counter securities

Initial public offerings

Global equities

Options

Fixed-income securities

Municipal bonds

U.S. government and agency bonds

Rollover IRAs

Certificates of deposit (CDs)

Corporate bonds

Convertible securities

Home equity line of credit

Mortgages

Cash flow and debt management

Education funding

Special situation planning, i.e., divorces, marriages, deaths

Business continuity planning

Retirement planning

Estate planning

Trusts

Unit investment trusts

Money market funds

Mutual funds

Futures

Managed futures

Precious metals

Active assets accounts

Margin accounts

Zero-coupon bonds

Individual retirement accounts (IRAs)

Roth IRAs

Education IRAs

SEP-IRAs

401(k) plans

Insurance

Pensions

Advisors who offer the above services are, in essence, comprehensive financial planners. If clients need something done that moves them closer to achieving their financial goals, it is the comprehensive financial planner's responsibility to help the client determine what must be done now and how best to go about achieving those goals. For example, if you are wondering how best to accumulate the money needed to send your children to college, what investment and tax strategies would work best for you, and the specific investment vehicles you should use, you can sit down with your financial advisor and discuss your options.

How Much Will this Trip Cost?

"I don't want to have to pay extra for services that I can get for a fraction of the cost." Why would any individual pay $200 for a stock trade that they could execute on their own for $10 or less? That is the question that has led to the boom in online trading and self-directed investment accounts.

The question of how a financial planner gets paid is a particularly important one as you establish a relationship with your planner. You do not want to be plagued by a nagging fear that your planner recommends products for the commissions they generate rather than for their appropriateness to your situation. In theory, financial planners have an ethical obligation to hold your financial interests above their own, but often how they are paid makes that philosophy difficult to execute. Planners are compensated in four basic ways:

Commission only. Such planners offer free consultation and profit only when you buy a product, such as a mutual fund, an annuity, or a life insurance policy. In some cases, the commissions are explicit—for example, a 4 percent front-end load on a mutual fund. In other cases, the fees are lumped into the general expenses of the product, as with life insurance, so you won't know how much your planner makes unless you ask. Because a planner who works on commission collects only if you buy, keep that in mind as you consider the planner's advice. When you interview such a planner, ask approximately what percentage of the firm's commission revenue comes from annuities, insurance products, limited partnerships, mutual funds, and stocks and bonds. The planner's answers will give you a sense of the kind of advice their firm usually gives.

Commissions are not only paid upfront, but also as ongoing charges that could apply as long as you hold that investment. In other cases, you must pay a fee if you sell a product before a particular amount of time has elapsed. If you sell certain mutual funds within one year of buying them, you must remit a back-end load, (See Chapter 3 for more on these.) If you want to cash in an annuity or insurance policy early, you must pay surrender charges of 7 percent or so of your investment, part of which reimburses the insurer for the commissions it has paid your planner.

Many commission-motivated planners also win prizes of merchandise or free travel if their sales of a particular product reach a target level. And soft-dollar arrangements award planners with non-cash goods and services, such as computer software, investment research, or magazine subscriptions, if their sales hit certain goals.

You should also ask about sales quotas, or if the advisor in any way is directed to recommend certain financial products over others. Salaries often depend on an advisor's ability to meet sales quotas; and quotas, incentives, and directives can lead to divided loyalties.

Though your planner might not like your questioning their cash payment and other perks, it is your right to know whether the products you buy generate direct income and other benefits for the planner. By knowing the full extent of your planner's compensation, you will be better able to decide whether the advice is objective or self-serving.

Fee only. Some professional planners assess your financial situation for a fee. Based on time spent with you, they either charge a flat dollar amount, or a percentage of your income or assets. Usually, such planners offer a no-cost, no-obligation initial consultation to explore your financial needs. They provide advice on how to implement their recommendations, but they do not collect a dime from commissions if you take their suggestions. The advantage of this arrangement, of course, is that the planner has no vested interest in having you buy one product over another because they do not stand to gain personally from any specific recommendation.

These planners therefore suggest no-load mutual funds or low-load life insurance policies that you probably would never hear about from a commission-oriented planner. The largest association of fee-only planners is the National Association of Personal Financial Advisors (NAPFA) in Arlington Heights, Illinois, which will supply a list of fee-only planners near you if you call the association at 888-FEEONLY.

The Garrett Planning Network, Inc. (GPN) (http://www.GarrettPlanning Network.com) is a nationwide network of fee-only financial planners dedicated to serving all Americans—not just the wealthy.

Fee and commission. The majority of financial planners charge some sort of fee for providing a financial plan but make most of their income from commissions on the products they sell. In some cases, such planners are actually captives of one company, so they recommend only its product line. Other such planners are independent and therefore recommend the mutual funds or insurance policies of a large number of companies with which they affiliate. However, because your planner earns a living by selling something to you, consider any advice warily, and try to determine a way to accomplish the same goals with lower priced products. Always consider total cost.

A variation on this form of compensation is called *fee offset,* which means that any commission revenue your planner earns from selling you products reduces the fee you pay for planning. If you buy so many products that your entire fee is covered, you deserve a refund or credit of the fee you paid for your basic plan.

Salary. Many banks, credit unions, savings and loans, and other organizations that offer financial planning provide the service through a salaried planner. While these planners do not have as strong an incentive to sell products as do commission oriented planners, they still steer you toward products offered by their financial institution, on which the institution earns a sales commission. If most of the salaried planner's clients execute their advice outside the bank or other financial institution, the planner probably will not keep the job for very long.

You also can search for planners at the Financial Planning Association Adviser Web site at http://www.fpanet.org. The FPA will send brochures explaining the financial planning process and how to select a financial advisor, an interview sheet to guide you through the selection process, and detailed background information on three advisors who match the criteria you specify.

▶ Setting Off on the Right Foot: Working with Your Advisor

The first meeting with your financial advisor will possibly be the most telling one of all. New clients typically decide whether they will do business with a specific financial advisor within the first few minutes of their meeting. First impressions do make a difference, and it is of the utmost importance that you feel at ease with your advisor from the very start. Money is a very personal and private matter.

Some people walk into that first meeting afraid that the financial professional will privately laugh at the poor job they have done of managing their money. Others walk in knowing they have done a superb job of accumulating a large amount of money and are afraid the advisor will try to change everything they have done. Neither of these apprehensions is warranted.

When you meet come prepared with any pertinent financial documents and a list of questions and concerns. The advisor will normally begin by asking, "What does your money mean to you?" and "What are your expectations for this money?" and will then proceed to a detailed financial questionnaire in an effort to understand the necessary financial information.

The advisor will then try to qualify and quantify your goals; for example, you might say "I want to put my children through college." The advisor will then work with you to determine what that means in dollars and cents: "I will need $100,000 in 15 years to fully fund my child's college tuition and other expenses."

Your financial advisor then evaluates the information and recommends a specific plan of action. *You* decide whether to implement the plan and can set up a schedule to monitor the plan on your own or with your advisor.

▶ Don't Go There: Investments to Avoid and Other Avoidable Errors

Whichever route you ultimately choose, there are several forms of savings and investments that are frequently touted as being ideal for college savings but are actually inappropriate. A few examples include cash value life insurance, annuities, limited partnerships, unit investment trusts, and highly speculative devices such as options or futures. All of these are designed to achieve other financial goals, such as insuring a life or providing retirement income, and therefore are inefficient and costly ways to pay for your children's college education.

Whether you invest in individual stocks and bonds or board the mutual fund train, make sure you avoid these common money management mistakes that can derail your plans:

▶ *Mistake 1: Not Diversifying.* To safeguard against problems should the industry or a specific company run into economic problems, don't keep more than about 10 percent of your total investments in any one stock (including your employer's stock!).

▶ *Mistake 2: Not Controlling Costs.* Unnecessary costs reduce investment returns. Do your own research on no-load, low-cost investment vehicles, or get advice from a fee-only financial advisor who charges by the hour.

▶ *Mistake 3: Paying Too Much Attention to Short-Term Results.* Which would you prefer: To know where the stock market will be in six months or six years? The smartest investors choose the longer-term outlook. Don't let day-to-day market fluctuations mesmerize you. Avoid the urge to buy "hot" stocks, last year's winning mutual fund, or this year's trendy sector fund. Don't expect some investment guru's newsletter to help you time the market's ups and downs.

Fluctuations in market value—including periodic bear markets—are a normal part of investing.

> *Time in the market, not market timing, is a major key to long-term investment success.*

▶ *Mistake 4: Not Sticking to Your Plan.* If you have a well-thought-out, long-term plan, don't get discouraged and abandon it after a market decline. You will lose out. You and/or your advisor should monitor your results on a quarterly and annual basis, but investment decisions should be made in a rational, unemotional way. Once you have made your portfolio decisions and set your asset allocation, stay the course until your goals and/or personal situation change. If the allocation percentages get out of balance, rebalance your holdings to bring the portfolio back to its proper weightings.

▶ *Mistake 5: Ignoring Tax Consequences.* Some investments (usually actively managed funds or investments that would generate capital gains taxes) are best sheltered in tax-advantaged accounts like 401(k)s and IRAs. Other tax-efficient investments, like index mutual funds and municipal bonds, can be held in taxable accounts. However, don't pay too much in account or policy costs just to defer taxes on the gains within these investments; for example, you do just that when you buy a high-cost variable annuity.

▶ *Mistake 6: Ignoring Investment History.* Although history does not necessarily repeat itself, there are patterns worth watching. The run-up, then collapse, of the Internet and technology bubble was just the most recent in a long line of boom/bust cycles. Studying historical trends can help you understand market cycles and volatility.

Roadmap 4.1

Evaluating the Performance of Your Portfolio

1. Determine your long-term financial goals, such as paying for a college education for your kids, or funding your retirement.
2. Carefully evaluate your tolerance for risk.
3. Allocate your assets.
4. Identify an index that has a close correlation to each asset class of your investment portfolio.
5. Assume that the best you will do over time is what the market does over the same period. Almost eighty percent of the efforts to beat the market fail.

At least once a year, measure the returns on your portfolio against those of the index that most accurately reflects its components. If the performance is as good as or better than the benchmark, you are on track. If the performance falls short of the benchmark, consider changing the investments that correspond to that asset class.

▶ *Mistake 7: Allowing Emotion to Rule.* Investing is about discipline—having a well-researched plan and sticking to it through thick and thin. Get-rich-quick or hit-it-big schemes are for casinos, not investing for your kid's college education.

▶ *Mistake 8: Not Protecting against Change.* In the current economic climate, interest rates, investment values, and inflation rates can change fairly quickly. While trade-offs are inevitable (risk/reward equations), a sound financial plan should seek to protect your principal and enhance your real rate of return throughout various economic conditions. Depending on individual circumstances and personal objectives, a diversified portfolio might include stocks and stock mutual funds, bonds and bond mutual funds, domestic and international equities. When one investment zigs, the others may zag.

▶ *Mistake 9: Not Saving Enough for Retirement.* Your retirement may last for 35 to 40 years. You can't depend on Social Security, so you need to build a substantial nest egg that takes into account variables like taxes, inflation, and health care costs, to name a few. The amount you need to save on a systematic basis will depend on your age, your expected life span, the current market value of your assets, and your personal goals and objectives (in this case planning for the funding of your child's college education). Remember there is no such thing as loans, grants, or work study for retirees. And sometimes we don't have a choice about when we have to retire.

▶ Setting Your Course: A Quick Review

As we've discussed, the final decisions about exactly how you should invest the money depend on lots of factors, including your time horizon, your risk tolerance, and what the rest of your investment portfolio looks like. None of these factors are especially complicated, but before we move on, let's take a moment to look back over where we've been.

Your Time Horizon. One key factor in determining how you'll invest depends on how much time you have before you'll need the money. If time is short and you have only five or six years to invest, you probably want to avoid stocks and other such investments, because you won't have time to ride out an extended drop in the financial markets. Instead, you probably want to focus on more stable investments, such as money market accounts, money market mutual funds, short-term Treasury securities (including inflation-indexed Treasury securities), and the like. You won't get the kind of return you might get through stocks and other equity investments, but you won't have to worry about the market's short-term performance. On the other hand, if you start saving when your child is young, you might want to avail yourself of the opportunities growth stocks or growth stock mutual funds afford.

Your Risk Tolerance. In general, the more risk you're willing to take, the greater your potential return. The less risk you're willing to take, the smaller your potential return.

Here's a general rule. If you have at least five to 10 years before you'll need to tap your account, go with a substantial portion of your portfolio in a diversified mix of stock mutual funds. This should give your account enough time to rebound from any extended drop in the market. However, if you'll need to tap your account sooner, stick with something stable.

Monitor Fees, Expenses. No matter how you decide to invest, watch out for commissions, fees and other expenses. Expenses can eat up a big portion of your earnings. As with other things, it pays to shop around.

Learn the Language

Key Terms to Know When Saving for College

Certified Financial Planner™ (CFP®) A designation of the Certified Financial Planner Board of Standards (CFP Board). CFPs have completed financial planning courses through a CFP-Board-registered college or university and a 10-hour two-day comprehensive exam covering financial planning, insurance, investing, taxes, retirement planning, employee benefits, estate planning, and risk management; must also have three years of qualifying work experience in the financial services industry and a defined amount of college education; must abide by the CFP code of ethics, and fulfill continuing education requirements.

Chartered Financial Analyst (CFA®) A designation of the Association for Investment Management and Research (AIMR). CFAs must demonstrate their expertise in investment valuation and management, asset valuation, portfolio management, and industry ethics by successfully completing their examinations and maintaining their expertise through continuing education; in addition they must have a bachelor's degree, adhere to the AIMR code of ethics, and have at least three years of work experience and a high level of professional conduct. CFAs are for those with a great amount of money to invest.

Chartered Financial Consultant (ChFC) A designation conferred by the American College. ChFCs must pass 10 college-level courses on all major topics of personal finance and business planning, possess industry experience, and adhere to strict ethical standards. To maintain the designation, they must obtain continuing education credits. Many ChFCs have particular expertise in life insurance matters.

Personal Financial Specialist (PFS) Only CPAs who are members of the AICPA are eligible. They must have at least three years of personal financial planning experience and demonstrate expertise by passing a comprehensive financial planning exam. A PFS concentrates on financial planning.

Where To Park Your Car

Choosing College Savings and Investment Vehicles

We've arrived at our destination. You have all the basic information about investments—individual stocks and bonds or mutual funds. You've decided to fly on your own or to assume the role of a co-pilot and work with a financial professional. Now, it's time for a brief look at some of the places where you might park that precious cargo—your child's college funds.

▶ Package Tours: Deciding Where to Put Your Cash

Just as there are many ways to invest for college, there are also a number of different types of accounts available to you. Each is designed to fit the needs of different families and different financial situations and each had its pluses and minuses. In this chapter we're going to take a look at the various routes you can travel.

Heading for College: Route 1—Custodial Accounts

Uniform Gifts to Minors Act (UGMA) and Uniform Transfers to Minors Act (UTMA) accounts are custodial accounts that can be set up to transfer assets to minors. The donor of the funds and the custodian of the account may or may not be the same person. UGMA/UTMA accounts must be used for the child's benefit and to cover expenses beyond normal parental obligations (definitions vary from state to state).

A UTMA is newer and more flexible than an UGMA. It can stay open for a longer time and more types of assets may be held in the account.

Eligible Investment Amounts. Individual donors can gift/transfer up to $11,000 per year per beneficiary. This amount is adjusted with inflation in $1,000 increments. Each citizen also has a lifetime exclusion amount (currently $1,000,000) that is above and beyond these annual exclusions. Exceeding the annual exclusion amount in any given year uses up part of the lifetime exclusion amount.

As an example, in a household with two parents and two minor children, in 2004 each parent could give each child $11,000 or a total of $44,000 per year. If the assets are titled in one parent's name, it is possible for that parent to give up to $22,000 per year to each child (no limits on transfers between spouses) without exceeding the exclusion amounts, provided that the spouse agrees to gift-splitting as defined by IRS rules (this will require filing a gift-tax return to document the split, although no tax will be owed).

One favorable exception to the $11,000 annual exclusion amount occurs with contributions to a Section 529 Savings Account where up to five years' worth of gifts can be combined into one year without exceeding the exclusion amounts. However, if any other gifts are made within those five years, they will use up part of the lifetime exclusion amount and you will be required to file a gift-tax return. Taxes may or may not be owed, depending on whether the entire lifetime exclusion amount has been used up.

UGMA/UTMA Basics

1. Unlike other methods of saving for college, there are no income or other eligibility limitations for UGMA/UTMA accounts.
2. Although the funds are in a custodial account, they are considered assets of the student and any distributions are considered student income. Thus, eligibility for need-based aid can be affected.
3. UGMA/UTMA funds can be used for any college expenses, including room and board, or non-college expenses of the beneficiary, like buying a car or funding a vacation.
4. The account custodian controls investment and disbursement until the child reaches the age of majority (18 or 21, depending on the state).

5. UGMA/UTMA account funds remain in the donor's estate if the donor is the custodian and dies before the child reaches the age of majority. From a transfer and estate planning perspective, it may make sense for someone other than the donor to be the custodian of the account.

Potential Candidates for This Approach to Savings

For some, these accounts are better for reducing the size of an estate than saving for college. UGMA/UTMA accounts can hurt financial aid eligibility and are taxed at a parent's tax rate until the child is 14.

If you have the money, a simpler approach may be to pay the student's tuition directly to the college. Such payments are excluded from the gift documentation and tax provisions and are not limited in amount. But that exclusion only applies to tuition.

Heading for College: Route 2– Series EE and Series I Bonds

Series EE savings bonds purchased after December 31, 1989, and the new Series I Inflation Protection Bonds are another way to pay for college and save on taxes. If the required conditions are met, the interest from these bonds is tax-exempt when used to pay for qualified educational expenses.

EE and I Bond Basics

1. Individuals can purchase up to $15,000 of Series EE bonds ($30,000 face value) and $30,000 (issued at face value) Series I bonds per year.
2. Bonds must have been issued after December 31, 1989, to receive preferential tax treatment; purchaser must be over 24 years old at the time of purchase; and bonds must be purchased in the parents' names. If bonds previously purchased are titled incorrectly, there is a procedure to get them retitled, provided that the parents initially purchased the bonds and the parents' income is below the eligibility limits at the time of redemption.
3. Redemption must be in the year of qualified expenses. Make certain your records include the bonds' serial number, face value, issue date, redemption date, total proceeds (principal and interest), receipt from the educational institution receiving the payment, and receipts for qualified expenses.

4. Interest on the bonds can be partially or completely tax-free, depending on the parents' income (indexed for inflation) in the year of redemption.

5. For tax purposes, bonds are considered a parental asset, and the interest is deemed income. The IRS adds redemption interest to your income before determining eligibility for the tax break, also affecting your adjusted gross income (AGI) for financial aid purposes.

6. Qualified expenses include tuition and fees but not room, board, and books.

7. Bond redemptions are reported on IRS forms 8815/8818.

8. Purchasing bonds in smaller denominations ($25 bonds rather than $1,000 bonds, for example) provides more flexibility, because any redemption amount that exceeds the amount of qualified expenses loses its tax-free treatment.

9. Bond's value is included in the bond owner's estate.

Savings bonds may appeal to families that expect to meet the income limitations at redemption, have a low risk tolerance and short time horizon, and, therefore, are willing to accept the relatively low but tax-free returns.

Heading for College: Route 3— Coverdell Education Savings Account

A Coverdell Education Savings Account (ESA), formerly called an Education IRA, is a kind of mini trust fund, or custodial account. It provides a wonderful way to accumulate savings that you may need to pay for your child's higher education because it allows you to deposit $2,000 per year per child under 18 into an IRA on a tax-deferred basis. This means that the money invested *does not* generate a deduction when placed in the ESA, but the principal and all income and capital gains can be withdrawn completely tax-free to pay for college expenses such as tuition, fees, books, even computer equipment, as well as room and board. (An added benefit is that you can now use the account to help pay expenses not only at college, but also at private and public elementary schools and high schools.)

ESAs are easy to set up at a bank, credit union, mutual fund company, discount brokerage company, or other financial institution and name a child or other minor as beneficiary. Before you sign up, make sure you read the plan agreement and disclosure statement carefully (the financial institution must give you copies), so that you'll fully understand any fees or other expenses that may be involved. Remember that fees and expenses reduce the amount that your account earns, so shop around for reasonable terms.

When you sign up, you'll name—or designate—the beneficiary of the account and provide a Social Security number and date of birth. You'll also name a responsible individual. This is generally the person who's in charge of the account and who decides how the money will be invested (after you make the initial choice). This person will also approve withdrawals from the account and decide whether to transfer the account to another member of the beneficiary's extended family should the need arise. Who you name as the responsible person listed on the account is your choice; it could be you. Check with the financial institution; it may allow you to name someone else.

If you're saving for a child's education, this is a great choice. It need not be the only thing you use; there are plenty of other vehicles out there, including the Section 529 plan (see below), but the ESA is definitely worth considering, even if it's just one of the ways in which you save.

If one child does not go to school, the ESA proceeds can be used for another child in the family who does attend college. The best way to invest money in an ESA is with growth vehicles such as growth-oriented mutual funds, because you will not pay taxes on capital gains, no matter how much the account grows, as long as you use the money to pay for college expenses.

Another related rule allows parents to withdraw money from regular IRAs before age 59½ without penalty if the proceeds are used for qualifying college or vocational school expenses. However, the money withdrawn must be reported as income in the year it is taken from the IRA. So the ESA is probably a better deal for those eligible to open one. If you do not use the assets in an ESA by the time your child is 30, the account must be liquidated and taxes paid on the proceeds at regular income tax rates.

ESA Basics

1. The contribution limit is $2,000 a year. You still may not be able to cover all of a child's education expenses, but you'll at least get a pretty good start.
2. You can qualify for tax-free and penalty-free withdrawals for all sorts of education expenses—including the cost of a computer, connecting to the Internet, and computer software and games (so long as they're educational in nature).

3. You can make tax-free withdrawals and claim other federal income tax breaks in the same year—through the HOPE and Lifetime Learning credits (assuming you're eligible)—as long as they're not all used for the same education expenses in the same year.

4. Contributions can be made in the same year for the same beneficiary to both an ESA and a state-sponsored college savings plan (Section 529 plan).

5. Excess contributions are subject to a 6 percent excise tax until they are withdrawn.

6. Life insurance contracts are not permitted.

7. Contributions can be made only if the beneficiary is less than 18 years old.

8. You have until the normal tax-filing deadline to make a contribution and have it count for the previous year. In other words, you generally have until April 15—the usual deadline for filing your federal income tax return—to invest money in an ESA and have it count for the previous tax year.

Who May Contribute? Just about anybody may contribute to an ESA. If you're saving for your child's or grandchild's education, that's fine. However, you may also contribute for somebody else: your niece, nephew, cousin—or your neighbor's newborn child; the beneficiary need not be related to you in any way; as long as you meet the income limits, you can open an account and start saving. In fact, as long as the beneficiaries are under 18 they can contribute on their own behalf.

Keep in mind that you're free to contribute to an ESA even if you don't have earned income (generally money from a job). However, there are income limits. That's one thing that makes these accounts somewhat unusual.

Income Limits on Contributors. The income limits for ESAs apply to the person or persons who are contributing the money, not to the beneficiary. The income limits are set fairly high. Still, they're out there, and they're a bit complicated. So, if your income is fairly high, and you're wondering whether you're eligible to contribute, you should know something about the limits and how they work.

When to Contribute. Although the law technically gives you until you file your tax return to make a contribution for the prior year, why wait? The sooner you get started, the more your account may earn. Suppose, for exam-

Hazard!

Education Savings Accounts Have Their Limits

Your current income affects whether you can participate in or benefit from any of these IRAs.

If your income falls below the range, you may contribute the maximum. If your income falls within the range, you may make a partial contribution but not the full amount. If your income falls above the range, you cannot make a contribution at all.

1. If you're single and your adjusted gross income (AGI) is below $95,000, you may contribute the full amount: $2,000. If your AGI is at or above $95,000 but less than $110,000, you may make a partial contribution. If your AGI is at or above $110,000, you can't contribute anything.
2. If you're married, filing a joint return, and if your AGI is below $190,000, you may contribute the full $2,000. If your AGI is at or above $190,000 but below $220,000, you may make a partial contribution. If your AGI is at or above $220,000, you can't contribute anything.

The income limits change periodically, so check with your tax advisor or IRS Publication 970, "Tax Benefits for Education," for the latest limits.

If you're above the income limits, it's acceptable for another individual who is not—for instance, a grandparent, friend, or even the child—to make the contribution. Just remember that the annual $2,000 contribution limit applies per beneficiary. No matter how many people may want to kick in each year—parents, grandparents, uncles, and aunts, for example—no more than $2,000 overall may be contributed in any single year for one beneficiary.

ple, that you plan to invest in an ESA for 2006. If you invest the full $2,000 in early January 2006 and earn 5 percent interest, your account will be worth $2,100 by early January 2007.

Can't afford to invest the full $2,000 in a lump sum in January 2006? You can also invest each month in 12 equal installments of about $166.67. At the end of the period, you'll wind up with about $2,055.

The point is that it's best not to delay, even though the law lets you. Start saving as soon as you can, so that your account can start earning money as soon as possible and you get the benefit of compounding. Not only can your principal earn interest, your interest can earn interest too, and all this on a tax-deferred basis.

Multiple ESAs. You may also contribute to more than one ESA. If you're a parent, for example, you may have one ESA for each child. If you're a grandparent, you may have one ESA for each grandchild. If you have five children, you may contribute $2,000 a year for each of them for a total of $10,000 in annual ESA contributions. Just be sure that no more than $2,000 is contributed on behalf of each beneficiary, no matter how many people contribute and no matter how many ESAs that beneficiary has.

In general, the shorter the time period during which you save, the smaller the potential benefit. The longer you save, the bigger the potential benefit. Suppose, for example, that your first child has just been born. You want to start saving immediately just in case you decide to enroll the child in a private elementary school in five years; if not you'll be getting a good jump on paying for that college education.

If you contribute $2,000 a year for five years, earning 7 percent a year, you wind up with about $11,500. If you forgo that elementary school and save until your child turns 18, you may be able to contribute $2,000 a year for over 19 years. Assuming you earn 7 percent a year, you end up with nearly $75,000. In other words, because you've saved for a longer period of time, your savings will have been allowed to grow on a tax-free basis all the while.

Students with Special Needs. There's one exception to the age 18 rule, and it deserves special note here: a beneficiary who has special needs. If you have a child who has a physical, mental, or emotional condition that requires special services, odds are you have enough on your mind without having to worry about college funding.

Nevertheless, medical, financial, and education counselors alike regularly stress the importance of developing a long-range financial plan for a child who has special needs—especially if the special needs will require years of extra care and attention.

If you're in this situation, consider making an Education Savings Account part of the child's long-term financial plan because the law has a number of unique provisions designed to offer help to people with special needs. For a special-needs beneficiary, for example, there is no age limit; you may contribute every year, and keep on contributing as long as the special-needs beneficiary is alive. Whatever is withdrawn from the account—original contributions as well as earnings—escapes tax and penalty, provided that it's used for the beneficiary's education expenses (which are broadly defined for special-needs beneficiaries).

Because of the unique benefits that an ESA offers, consider using one as part of the long-term financial plan for a child with special needs. Bear in mind that, in general, you may make tax-free and penalty-free withdrawals from an ESA on behalf of a special-needs beneficiary to pay for tuition, fees, tutoring, special needs services, room and board, uniforms, books, supplies, computers, and other equipment. "Supplementary" items or services, such as extended-day programs at a public or private elementary, middle, or high school are also included in the list. You may use the money tax-free and penalty-free for most types of college expenses, too.

Tax Consequences of ESAs. If you run afoul of the rules, you run into a tax mess, so stick to the rules, which isn't hard to do. Just use the money that's in the account for the purposes described as education expenses, and you're all set. The money you withdraw from the account will be free of tax and penalty.

Here's the general principle: If your withdrawal is equal to or less than the education expenses, you have no problem. If your withdrawal is greater than the education expenses, you face tax trouble.

The Rollover Option. If, for example, your child decides not to go to college, you may roll over the money from one beneficiary's ESA to the ESA of another beneficiary in your extended family. Moving the money to the ESA of another beneficiary who's in the same family lets you escape tax and penalty. The point is to use the money for the purpose that Congress intended: education. If you can't use or use up all the money you've saved in one beneficiary's ESA, you can move it to another beneficiary's ESA where it can be used up—without triggering tax or penalty.

How Rollovers Work: Rollovers come into play in two key ways: when you want to move money and when you must move money. Once you open an Education Savings Account with a trustee or custodian (typically a financial institution), remember that you're not locked in. You are free to move the money to another financial institution; however, there may be costs involved. You're not limited to just one ESA trustee or custodian; you may move your ESA from one place to another—from a bank to a brokerage, for example, or from a mutual fund company to a credit union.

You'll have to do the same sort of research you did when you first opened your account, comparing such factors as fees, interest rates, investment flexibility, and investment performance. Another factor to weigh is whether the trustee you plan to leave (and the trustee you plan to move to) will charge some kind of account-closing fee and how much you might have to pay.

You may do a rollover not just to an account for the benefit of the same beneficiary, but also for the benefit of another beneficiary (who's a member of the same extended family). To avoid tax consequences, you may transfer or roll over the money from one ESA to another ESA of another qualified recipient.

Rules for Rollovers: You may roll over the money from one ESA to another without tax consequences. Rolling over money generally means that you withdraw it from one ESA and deposit or invest in another. But rollovers have strict limits. For example:

1. You must complete a rollover within 60 days to avoid tax trouble. The clock starts ticking the day you withdraw the money.
2. You're allowed only one rollover per ESA during any 12-month period. This is a rolling 12-month clock, not a calendar year. If you withdraw money from an ESA on November 1 for a rollover, you can't do another rollover before November 1 of the following year.

Special Situations

There are some other special situations you should be aware of.

If a spouse or former spouse receives the ESA under a divorce or separation agreement, there's no tax consequence. After the transfer, the spouse (or former spouse) gets to treat the ESA as their own. The ESA's beneficiary can be changed, and the beneficiary's interest in the account can be transferred to a spouse (or former spouse) as a result of the divorce.

In general, you may roll over an ESA from one beneficiary to another only if the new beneficiary is under age 30. However, if the new beneficiary is a special-needs beneficiary, age won't matter; the rollover can be made without fear of tax consequences.

Heading for College: Route 4– Section 529 Plans Overview

Qualified tuition plans, also known as 529 Plans, are a popular education savings method that feature special tax benefits and allow significantly greater contributions than other options like the Coverdell Education Savings Account. Every state and the District of Columbia now has at least one 529 Plan. With so many choices, it's important to know the basics about how these plans work and what to consider before you invest.

How 529 Plans Work. Anyone—parents, relatives, and friends—can contribute money to a 529 Plan on behalf of a beneficiary (student), and, unlike Coverdell ESAs, contributors are not subject to income limitations, nor are there restrictions on the beneficiary's age. The only requirement is that amounts accumulated in the plan must be used to pay for the qualified education expenses of an undergraduate or graduate program at an accredited institution. Expenses that qualify include tuition, fees, books, supplies, required equipment, and room and board.

The Two Types of 529 Plans: Prepaid and Savings

Prepaid plans. With prepaid tuition plans, which allow you to prepay college tuition bills years in advance, you fund future tuition costs—and *only* tuition costs—by purchasing college credit hours at today's rates to a particular college which the child must attend. When the credit hours are used, the plan pays the going rate for tuition at the time your child attends the school. Because the sponsoring state generally guarantees prepaid plans (although some state plans don't provide an ironclad guarantee), you are usually assured the tuition money will be there when you need it.

Savings plans. In these plans, your contributions are invested in mutual funds offered by the plan's program manager (like Vanguard, TIAA-CREF, or Fidelity). Some plans allow you to choose among different investments or investment portfolios. Most have ready-made investment portfolios tailored to age and risk tolerance, and these are professionally managed by the state or program manager.

Remember that investments in 529 Savings Plans fluctuate with the stock and bond markets, so they need to be monitored regularly just like retirement savings and other investments. You can change your investment selections in a plan or move the plan assets to another state's plan once a year.

Requirements and Benefits. Both types of 529 Plans are subject to the requirements of the sponsoring state, though many states allow nonresidents to participate in their plans.

Among the benefits of a 529 Plan are

1. *No federal income tax.* According to section 529 of the Internal Revenue Code (how 529 Plans got their name), earnings from plan investments are free from federal income tax, as long as the funds are used to pay for qualified education expenses.

2. *State tax deductions.* Some states allow a deduction for contributions to the state's 529 Plan, others may tax out-of-state Plan contributions, and still others follow the federal rules.
3. *Estate planning advantages.* A powerful estate planning tool, 529 Plans allow individuals to make gifts of $11,000 annually to anyone without reporting the contribution or paying a federal gift transfer tax. Under a special provision of the plan rules, an individual can contribute up to $55,000 in one year to the plan without triggering the gift tax. The election treats the gift as if it had been $11,000 per year over a five-year period. The only requirement is that no further gifts be made to that person for the next five years. A married couple can gift up to $110,000 per beneficiary in one year and reduce their taxable estate. A portion of the gift may be included in your taxable estate if you die within the five-year period.

These benefits, coupled with large contribution maximums (the maximum in 529 Savings Plans is now $235,000 in some states; the contribution to prepaid plans is in the range of $50,000 to $100,000), make 529 Plans attractive savings and asset transfer vehicles. However, if you use the money for anything other than qualified education expenses, you face a 10 percent penalty tax and tax on the earnings subject to that distribution. Special exceptions apply if the student receives a scholarship, dies, or becomes disabled.

Choosing a 529 Plan. Some considerations when deciding on a plan include the following:

1. *Eligibility.* Is the plan fully open to nonresidents?
2. *Fees and expenses.* Is there a sales commission, an enrollment fee, or annual maintenance fee? Is there an asset-based management fee? What are the annual expenses of the underlying investments?
3. *Investment considerations.* Does the plan use age-based or years-to-enrollment portfolios? Is there a fixed or guaranteed investment option? Can you build your own investment portfolio? How often can you change your investments? Who manages the plan investments?
4. *Contributions.* What are the minimum initial and subsequent contributions allowed by the plan? What is the maximum contribution allowed? How much is deductible on my state income tax return?

5. *Time or age limitations.* Is there any limit on the age of the account beneficiary? How long can the account stay open? Are there restrictions on withdrawing funds from the plan?

A final consideration is the plan's impact on need-based financial aid. Prepaid plans are considered a student asset and result in a dollar-for-dollar reduction in financial aid. However, 529 Savings Plans are considered the owner's asset, not the beneficiary's. If the owner is the parent, up to 6 percent of the account's value will be included in the financial aid formulas. Private colleges may treat these plans as a student asset, which will be assessed at 25 percent for financial aid formulas.

In general, 529 Plans tend to be most appropriate for families who do not expect to qualify for financial aid or who do not want to count on financial aid. Visit http://www.savingforcollege.com for up-to-date information on all 529 Plans available.

Heading for College: Exit 4A–Section 529 Prepaid Tuition Plans

Not all states offer prepaid tuition plans. At the time of writing this, 17 states offer *both* prepaid tuition plans and college savings plans (described above).

If you pay with either a lump sum or a series of payments, your child is guaranteed up to four years (if you prepaid that many credit hours) at a state school when they reach college age, no matter what the tuition at that time. The price of college is deeply discounted; the younger your child, the steeper the discount. These plans can be a good deal if you are fairly sure that your child will want to attend college in your state.

Prepaid tuition plans do have some drawbacks. If your child attends school out of state, each program has different refund policies. Some states will refund the equivalent of current state tuition. Others will give back only your initial investment, plus a low rate of interest. Some will refund only your initial investment without interest and also hit you with a cancellation fee. In addition, the IRS has ruled that you must pay federal income tax on the difference between your initial investment and the cost of tuition covered by another state's prepaid tuition plan when your child enrolls.

Many states also offer savings programs in which your money is invested and grows tax-deferred inside a trust according to the tax rules of IRS Section 529. Most states invest the money very conservatively in Treasuries and

CDs and offer a guaranteed floor rate of return of 3 or 4 percent, while others put at least some of the assets in stocks, offering higher return potential but also more risk. In these plans, assets are kept in the parent's name but are taxed at the child's more advantageous tax rate when the child attends college. If the child decides not to go to school, the assets can be used for other children who do. If the money is not used for college education, the parents can take it back, though they would pay taxes on the money and have to fork over a 10 percent penalty as well. So it is best to sign up for such a program only if you are fairly sure that your child will use the money for college expenses in your state.

 Tollbooth 5.1

Comparison of Education Savings Accounts (ESA) and 529 Savings Plans

Feature	ESA	529 Plan
Taxation of earnings if used for education	Not taxed	Not taxed*
Deductibility of contributions on federal and state taxes	No/No	No/Maybe (varies by state)
Annual contribution limit**	$2,000	None (subject to lifetime limits)
Subject to income limits	Yes (see above)	No
Beneficiary age restrictions	Yes (see above)	No
Can be used for grades K-12	Yes	No
Investment restrictions (generally)	Few	Many (varies by state)
Student asset or parent asset in financial aid formula***	Student	Parent
Revocable contributions	No	Yes

*If current rules are not extended, distributions after December 31, 2010, will be taxed at the beneficiary's tax rate.

**Gift tax rules apply; 529 plan has a special five-year gifting provision.

***Federal formula counts 529 assets as the parent's; some private colleges may count 529 assets as the student's; need-based financial aid may be affected.

Eligible Investment Amounts. These vary by state but generally are large enough to cover the expense of four years of college. State-by-state comparisons and investment amounts are available at http://www.finaid.org/savings/state529plans.html.

Prepaid Tuition Plan Basics

1. Some states require owner or beneficiary residency.
2. Annual distributions may affect financial aid eligibility.
3. Eligible expenses vary by state.
4. State maintains investment control.
5. Nonqualified withdrawals are subject to income tax plus a 10 percent penalty.
6. The original contribution is usually refundable to the contributor subject to taxes and penalty, although interest may be lost.

Prepaid tuition plans may appeal to families with young children or those not likely to qualify for need-based financial aid.

Independent 529 Plan. Hundreds of colleges offer a more limited form of prepaid tuition plan, often known as a tuition discount program. These programs allow you to pay for four years of tuition in a lump sum when your child enrolls as a freshman. Most schools will lend you the money to participate in this program. Interest rates vary widely. You might take advantage of this program if you think the school's tuition will rise faster than the interest rate on the loan and if the interest rate is competitive to one you could obtain elsewhere, such as on a home-equity loan.

Heading for College: Exit 4B–
Section 529 College Savings Plans

As we said, each state designates a particular investment company or two to offer plans to that state's residents, though you can also invest in plans from other states. Among the firms that states have chosen to offer these plans are American Century, Fidelity, Merrill Lynch, Putnam, Smith Barney, Strong, TIAA-CREF, T. Rowe Price, and Vanguard.

The firm invests the money in the account for you. In some states, you have a choice of investment alternatives; in other states, the manager makes all investment decisions for you. In some states, you choose between aggressive, moderate, or conservative tracks. In other states, the investment manager will invest aggressively from the time your child is born to about age 10 and then invest increasingly conservatively until the money is in a money-market fund by the time it is needed for tuition bills.

Contributions to the Section 529 Plan are tax deductible for the donor in some states and not others. In some states, the plan matches part of your contribution.

A special provision of the 529 Plan allows contributions to be averaged for gift-tax purposes over a five year period, so you can contribute up to $55,000 ($110,000 if married) to a beneficiary's account in one year without triggering any gift-tax implications.

Most colleges count 529 Plan assets as the account holders', not beneficiary's, assets when computing financial aid. However, any dollar amount spent from the plan for your child's education will be considered the student's income.

If your first child decides not to go to college, the assets can be transferred to a second child and still retain any tax benefits. If you withdraw the money for noneducational purposes, you will be hit with a 10 percent penalty and have to pay income taxes on the money you take out.

Saving for College: Route 5– Variable Universal Life Insurance

The challenge of saving and paying for a child's college education has given rise to a cottage industry of businesses offering advice, services, and products to help families overcome the obstacles in saving for college. In turn, that's led to some creative strategies to potentially enhance the prospects of qualifying for financial aid. Some are effective; others are not. Variable Universal Life insurance is one of those more creative strategies that can be appropriate in very unusual circumstances.

To evaluate whether Variable Universal Life (VUL) insurance is the right college savings vehicle, you should consider the following points:

Your Need for Life Insurance. First and foremost, VUL is life insurance. Do you have a genuine need for it? If not, VUL may not be the best savings vehicle.

Your Tolerance for Risk. VUL is a permanent insurance policy, unlike term insurance. VUL has a death benefit and a savings element or cash value.

With a VUL product, the policy's cash values typically are invested in a mix of mutual fund-like sub-accounts that allow policyholders to save for their children's anticipated college expenses. Keep in mind, though, the policy's cash value is directly affected by the performance of the sub-accounts. A VUL may be a poor choice for investors who cannot stomach the risk of potential market decline or do not have enough time horizon to recover from periodic investment setbacks.

Financial Aid Implications. A dependent student's financial aid eligibility is based on both the parents' and the student's assessable income and assets. Parents' income is assessed at rates up to 47 percent, the student's income at 50 percent. Parents' assets typically are assessed at 5.6 percent and the student's at 35 percent. The sum total of all this is the Expected Family Contribution (EFC). If it's less than the Cost of Attendance, the student has a financial need. A decrease in either income or assets of parents or the student lowers the EFC, increases the student's financial need, and (presumably) increases the amount of aid awarded.

Some of the more creative strategies in college financial planning have evolved as a way to exploit this formula. VUL is a good example. Life insurance cash values generally are not assessed in the financial aid calculation, but liquid savings are. A solution might be to save in the VUL. Moreover, withdrawals from the VUL (to pay for tuition, for example) are not treated as income, thereby lowering total assessable income in the years during which the student is attending college and applying for aid.

Note: Many private colleges use their own aid calculations and their discretion in assessing policy cash values, so transferring lots of cash into a life insurance policy is no guarantee that those values won't be assessed.

Policy Costs. Life insurance policies are complex products with varying levels of costs and expenses. All life insurance policies carry a charge for the underlying death benefit. Most carry additional administrative fees. Many, VUL included, impose charges on or against the value of the cash account. Also, many states levy a tax or surcharge on policy premiums. All these charges easily can eat up the expected benefit from a financial aid perspective. Therefore, any decision to use VUL as a savings vehicle, predicated on an expected increase in financial aid, must include an analysis of the cost of the policy and its expected return versus the cost of your other options.

Additional Considerations

Taxes. Saving for college via life insurance avoids income taxes on gains in the cash value. Withdrawals from cash value to pay tuition usually are structured as withdrawals up to the policyholder's basis in the contract, then as a loan against any gains in the policy cash value. As long as the contract is not surrendered, the loans are not taxable to the recipient. If the policy remains in force at the time of the insured's death, the loan balance is subtracted from the death benefit payable to the beneficiary.

Fees. If you change your mind or no longer need the life insurance, getting out of a VUL policy can be expensive. Life insurance policies sold by brokers or agents often carry steep surrender fees for the first five to 10 years. Consider buying a no-load or low-cost VUL policy instead.

Note: VUL's cousin, variable annuities are insurance contracts whose value fluctuates with that of its underlying securities portfolio. Like a VUL policy, the variable annuity's value is not included among either the parents' or the student's assets, potentially increasing prospects for financial aid. One popular and potentially very costly and dangerous strategy is for parents to take out a home equity loan (private colleges assess the parents' home equity when determining aid eligibility), then use the proceeds to fund a variable annuity. All the considerations that apply to the VUL as a savings vehicle also apply to variable annuities. But, unlike with a VUL, withdrawals from a variable annuity are not treated as loans, and the earnings are subject to taxes at ordinary income tax rates. What's more, withdrawals from a variable annuity before the owner reaches age 59½ are subject to a 10 percent federal income tax penalty.

Hazard!
Lying on Aid Applications

Under no circumstances is it appropriate for parents to lie about or misrepresent the true amount of their assets and/or income when submitting a college financial aid application. Material misrepresentations regarding the nature and amount of the applicant's or the parents' assets or income can result in severe legal and civil penalties.

▶ Ticketing: Whose Name Should Appear on the Account?

As we have just seen, whoever is considered owner of the account can have great consequences in terms of control, taxes, and financial aid. Under the present tax laws, it often no longer makes sense for parents to fund college trusts because all assets in a child's name are taxed at the parent's rate if the child is under 14 years of age. Once the beneficiary turns 14, all earnings are again taxed at the child's rate.

As a result of this rule, if you choose to go with a UGMA/UTMA you should fund the account with investments that produce little, if any, taxable income but provide long-term capital growth. Growth stock mutual funds are appropriate investments for your child's account, as are municipal bonds or municipal bond funds, which pay tax-exempt interest.

Putting assets in your child's name has some disadvantages. Once the child reaches the age of 18, the money in the UGMA account is completely at their disposal and they can choose how to use the money. Therefore, if your child spends it on a sports car instead of college tuition, bad luck! You can't do anything about it. You hope your child would never squander all this carefully invested capital, but how would you predict that by looking at your two-year-old now?

Another downside of building up a child's portfolio is that if your child applies for financial aid, the college will require that a high percentage of the assets—usually about 35 percent—be used to pay for tuition. In contrast, colleges insist that parents spend only about 6 percent of their assets for their child's college costs. Therefore, if you want to be totally in control and able to have your child qualify for the maximum amount of financial aid, keep all college funds in your name, and pay tuition bills out of your account.

For these reasons a Section 529 Savings Plan, which is a savings plan sponsored by an individual state, leaves you in control. In addition, all earnings are tax-free, if the proceeds are used for qualified education expenses. Although you name the account's beneficiary, the account remains yours to use if needed; however, you may pay a penalty to do so. In addition, you may change the beneficiary at any time. Although you still technically own and control the account, your contributions are considered a gift to the beneficiary.

▶ College or Bust: Estate Planning and Funding Your Child's Education

For many people, education is an important aspect of life. Parents want to see their children get an education, and grandparents want to ensure that their grandchildren get an education. Should you die when your children or grandchildren are very young or before they finish their education, the provisions you include in your estate plan can make all the difference to them, so consider them very carefully.

People define the word *education* in different ways. When you are drawing up your will or setting up trusts, make sure you elaborate on what the word means to you. Does it mean, for example, only higher education, and if so does it include graduate school? Conversely, does it mean private preschool, elementary, and secondary schools? If you don't make your intentions clear, your wishes may be contested or may not be carried out.

What do you mean when you say you want to pay for education? How sure are you that your definition matches your lawyer's definition of education? Ask yourself these questions:

1. Does education mean education at any level? Do private elementary school and high school count? Does it include a master's, doctorate, or some other postgraduate degree? Does it apply to vocational as well as academic institutions?
2. Do payments for education include room and board (on campus or off campus)? Books (new or used)? A computer (what type)? Transportation expenses (around campus or only to and from home at break)?
3. Are there any additional conditions or restrictions? Can the funds be used to pay for multiple degrees at the same level (e.g., three bachelor's degrees)? Does a particular grade point average need to be maintained? What about a certain number of credit hours per semester?

It may seem silly now, but it can make all the difference later.

Remember, once you have decided what is important to you, your will or trust must reflect your intentions. You need to make sure your lawyers know what you believe, what you value, and what you intend your estate plans to accomplish. Then, you need to read what they write and make sure you understand what it says. You will not be there to correct misinterpretations. You do not want people to think you value, say, a college education, when you actually believe that college degrees are overrated. Your estate plan is your voice after your death. You need to make sure it speaks the words you intend. It also helps if you foster those values in your beneficiaries. Please read *On the Road: Planning an Estate* for in-depth information on this topic.

Snorkeling for Hidden Treasures

Financial Aid and Other Sources of Money

Even if you have saved diligently and amassed a large college fund—and particularly if you haven't been so conscientious—you will likely need to apply for financial aid to cover at least part of your children's college costs. Many grants, loans, scholarships, and other programs exist, some offering better opportunities than others, including need-based, merit-based, private financial aid, and tuition discounts. Obviously, not everyone will qualify for each of these, but, before rejecting any mode of travel, it's important to investigate each type.

1. *Need-Based Financial Aid* is the most common form of aid, and it comes from federal or state governments or from private colleges and universities. Packages can include low-interest loans, grants (money that does not have to be repaid), and/or work-study programs.

2. *Merit-Based Financial Aid* is given to a student for outstanding performance in a particular area such as athletics, the arts, or academics. Many prestigious schools offer very little merit-based aid compared

with their second- and third-tier counterparts. Athletic scholarships, for example, are limited to NCAA Division I and II schools. Smaller liberal arts schools tend to be NCAA Division III—and are not allowed to award athletic scholarships.

3. *Private Financial Aid.* Recipients of private aid often satisfy particular requirements set forth by the sponsoring organization, and it often takes research to find these scholarships. Community organizations like the local PTA, garden club, Lions Club, and more give out this type of aid.

4. *Tuition Discounts.* These are unique to each school, and you won't know about them until you ask. Colleges and universities determine whether your child is eligible for need-based aid from your responses to the Free Application for Student Aid (FAFSA), and/or the PROFILE, and possibly their own unique forms.

Let's begin by looking at the types of grants available and then explore some additional and alternative ways to finance a child's education. Next, we'll help guide you through the maze of the aid application process, and last, but definitely not least, we'll take a look at the bright side—the tax incentives the government provides to help you pay the fare.

▶ Win a Cruise: Grants

Begin your search for financial aid with grants, which cost you nothing and do not have to be repaid. The most common sources of grants follow:

Port-of-Call 1: Pell Grants

Pell grants are given mostly to students in low-income families. For the 2004–05 award year, the grants ranged from about $400 to as much as $4,050 a year (but change based on funding), with the higher amount reserved for the families with minimal assets and earnings. To determine whether your child is eligible for a Pell grant, calculate your expected family contribution (EFC) using the standard formula reproduced on the application for the grant. If your EFC is low enough, your child might receive a grant. (More detailed information on EFC can be found in the next section.)

To calculate the amount of your Pell grant, subtract your EFC from the maximum authorized Pell grant, currently $4,050. The grant will depend somewhat on the cost of tuition at your child's school, whether your child will be a full- or part-time student, or will attend school for a full academic year. The child should apply for a Pell grant even if they know that it would be difficult to get one, because colleges normally won't consider a student for another grant unless they have been rejected for a Pell. For more information on the Pell grant application process, call 800-4-FED-AID.

Port-of-Call 2: Supplemental Educational Opportunity Grants (SEOGs)

These grants are funded by the federal government and administered through college financial aid offices. The grants to undergraduates range from $100 to $4,000 a year, with larger amounts of money going to lower income students. The priority goes to those receiving Pell grants. SEOG funds are limited, so it is important to submit an application as early as possible. Each school sets its own deadlines for campus-based funds, and those deadlines are usually earlier than the Department of Education's deadline for filing a FAFSA (Federal Supplemental Educational Opportunity Grant), which is usually sometime in June.

Port-of-Call 3: State Programs for Residents

Most states provide student grants based on a combination of merit and financial need. To be eligible for some grants, your child must meet a certain academic threshold, such as a B average. Your family's financial status is considered next. Other grants are made solely on academic accomplishment, no matter what your family's level of need. Your child's high school guidance counselor should know the details of grants available in your state.

Port-of-Call 4: College Grants and Scholarships

Most institutions offer several kinds of grants, which may or may not be based on financial need. Many merit scholarships are awarded purely on superlative high school academic achievement and high SAT test scores. Some colleges give cash grants, while others offer tuition discounts. Colleges also award grants to athletes, musicians, and others with special skills that the schools prize.

Port-of-Call 5: Private Grants and Scholarships

Thousands of grants and scholarship programs are available to students with superior academic records, special interests, and other qualifying characteristics. The National Merit Scholarship program awards grants purely on academic performance. Some grants are given by companies to their employees' children; others, by the local chamber of commerce. Some trade groups offer scholarships to students wanting to pursue careers in the groups' industries.

Many companies offer scholarship programs for the children of employees, as well as various contests that offer thousands of dollars toward college tuition. In addition, many companies reimburse most or all of an employee's tuition if the courses relate to the employee's current or future career. Some even reimburse employees for courses unrelated to their job; typically, they reimburse 50 percent of the tuition for unrelated courses. If your child is thinking of working through college, working for a company with a good tuition program is a big plus.

Different companies set varying requirements for tuition reimbursement. Some firms insist only that you pass the course; others reimburse you according to your grade (100 percent for an A, 80 percent for a B, etc.). In some cases, employers pay the school directly; in other cases, you must put out your own money, and your firm will reimburse you at the end of the term, when you prove that your child has completed the course satisfactorily.

If you receive education assistance, it is not considered taxable income unless your tuition bills exceed $5,250 per year. If you spend your own money on books, lab fees, tutors, travel, or other extras, you may be able to take a personal deduction on your tax return if your employer does not reimburse you for those costs.

Other forms of education assistance that employers provide are cash awards, scholarships, loans, and grants. Your company might pay for you to attend business school, for example, and also grant you paid or unpaid leave to complete the program.

To locate private grants or scholarships for which your child may be eligible, consult some of the books listed in Appendix B. You may want to consult a scholarship search service or other similar services with Web sites that will send you, for a fee, a printout of grants and scholarships that your child may be eligible to receive.

You must be careful about claims made by many commercial scholarship search services. The Federal Trade Commission has launched Project $cholar$cam to alert consumers about potential fraud in this arena and how to avoid it (See Roadmap 6.1 for six signs of scholarship scams). The FTC's

FTC's Six Warning Signs of Scholarship Scams

1. "Scholarships are guaranteed or your money back." No one can legitimately guarantee you will receive a scholarship or grant, and refunds may be difficult to get.
2. "You can't get this information anywhere else." There are a multitude of books, Web sites, and other resources; some of these are listed in Appendix B.
3. "Please give me your credit card number so I can hold this scholarship for you." Since no one can guarantee you will get a scholarship, it is dangerous to give your credit card number over the phone.
4. "We'll do all the work for you." Services may be able to identify potential scholarships, but you or your child has to write the essay and fill out the application to win the money.
5. "This scholarship will cost you some money." No one can hold a scholarship or grant for a fee. You win the grant because of your qualifications, not because you pay for it.
6. "You've been selected by a national foundation to receive this scholarship." It is highly unlikely that a foundation has selected you if you did not apply in the first place. In the same vein, be suspicious if someone told you that you have won a contest that you don't remember entering.

Web site on the subject can be found at http://www.ftc.gov/bcp/conline/edcams/scholarship/psa.htm.

If your child is awarded a grant or scholarship, the college will deduct that amount from the financial aid it would otherwise give your child, as required by federal rules, because the award is considered a source of income, and parents must declare all sources of income when applying for loans. Nevertheless, the scholarship could save you money if you wouldn't have qualified for much financial aid. Or if the college awards your child a grant, the scholarship can reduce the amount you must borrow.

▶ Passports, Visas, and Other Travel Documents: Winning the Financial Aid Game

The premise is simple: To receive financial aid, a student must prove that the family needs the money. To determine how much, a standard *needs analysis* examines what the parents can afford to pay and what the student can contribute. Financial aid is designed to supplement, not replace, a family's contribution to college costs. Therefore, all institutions expect a family to pay their fair share.

The factors that determine how much financial aid a family qualifies for include the parents' and student's income and assets, the size of the family, and the number of children attending college. The more income and assets a family has, the more college costs it is expected to pay. The financial aid forms you obtain from the school your child wants to attend will help you go through the application process step by step. (The FAFSA form is available online, too.)

Public and private schools use the FAFSA to allocate federal aid. Private colleges often require the PROFILE (and sometimes their own form) to determine how money is allocated. To apply for financial aid, you should complete these forms before January of your child's senior year of high school—and then every year while the child is in college.

The two types of forms result in two general financial aid formulas—the Federal Methodology and the Institutional Methodology, with many versions of the latter, because private colleges can decide what questions you must answer on the PROFILE (in section Q) and how they will treat that information. In general, both methodologies collect information about the parents' income and assets, the child's income and assets, how many people are in the family and their ages, and whether both parents work.

Some differences in the two methodologies can result in different expected family contributions (EFCs). For example, the Federal Methodology doesn't include the equity in your home, but the Institutional does. The Federal Methodology includes the value of your personal property (cars and more) or any loans, but the Institutional may or may not. Neither formula has traditionally included parents' qualified retirement plans and IRAs, but some anecdotal evidence suggests that private colleges may be starting to do so.

The result of these calculations is your EFC, which is the amount that your family is expected to pay for one year of college. For example, a family of four with one child in college and one not yet in college, an annual income of $75,000, and no savings might have an EFC of $8,000 per year. Although public universities and private colleges calculate their EFCs somewhat differently, the results generally are in the same ballpark, with the EFC at private colleges generally higher than at public universities. How much need-based financial aid this hypothetical child might qualify for depends on the cost of the college.

	PRIVATE COLLEGE	PUBLIC UNIVERSITY
Cost of Attendance	$27,700	$12,800
– EFC	8,000	8,000
= Financial Need	$19,700	$ 4,800

The child could be eligible for up to $19,700 in need-based financial aid at a private school, compared with up to $4,800 at a public institution. Keep in mind that, at both schools, at least a portion of any aid is likely to come in the form of a student loan and work-study program, in addition to possible grant money.

> *Just because a student qualifies for a certain amount of need-based aid doesn't mean a school must provide that amount.*

Applying for Your Passport: Financial Aid

The process of applying for financial aid can be daunting. You must fill out several confusing forms and provide a detailed profile of your financial situation to colleges, federal agencies, banks, and other lenders. The entire ordeal is so strenuous that an industry of financial aid counselors has emerged to help you work through the procedure—for a fee that can run several hundred dollars. Before you contact such a consultant, however, give the financial aid application process a try.

If you have completed Roadmaps 2.1 and 2.2, Assets and Liabilities Worksheets, they'll be handy now. If you haven't done them yet, now is a good time. Once you've determined your net assets, deduct the amount of money your family needs to live, which includes a certain allocation to savings. The remainder, known as the *parental contribution,* is the amount you are expected to spend for college tuition and expenses.

Once you determine the cost of tuition, room and board, and other fees and expenses, apply your parental contribution—plus any money your child can pay out of their income or assets—to the total school costs. Whatever remains is considered your family's financial need.

The FAFSA is the application used by virtually all colleges and universities to determine a student's financial aid eligibility using the Federal Methodology (FM) need analysis formula based on most recent year tax return information and other demographic (for example, family size, married or divorced, or single parent) and financial information.

Private schools use different formulas to determine financial need. Major determining factors include income, assets, family size, and number of family members in college. Special circumstances may also be given consideration, and the college may exercise its professional judgment to adjust the calculated parental contribution.

So, for example, your child might qualify for more aid if unusual circumstances, such as a recent divorce, job loss, or unusual medical expenses, can be documented. If you or your child explains why your family's situation is exceptional in a well-crafted letter, you might receive more aid than the guidelines normally allow. Financial aid officers may have some flexibility in dispensing their own school's funds, but not federal funds.

You can take a few other steps to improve your child's financial aid package.

When completing the aid applications, be honest, but don't overstate the value of family assets because it will reduce the amount of aid for which your child qualifies. For example, be conservative when estimating the value of your home. You can also invest money in retirement plans, such as individual retirement accounts (IRAs), Keogh plans, and 401(k) salary reduction plans, because you do not report these assets on Federal Methodology financial aid forms (although this may be changing).

It's also a good idea not to sell assets such as stocks, bonds, or mutual funds in the year before you apply for aid because any capital gains those sales generate are reported on your tax return, which will be used when applying for aid. Capital gains are counted as income and weigh more heavily against you than do assets in the assessment of need.

Mail in the financial aid application—which might include the Free Application for Federal Student Aid (FAFSA), the CSS/Financial Aid PROFILE form from the College Board's College Scholarship Service, the Family Financial Statement (FFS) from ACT, Inc. (formerly the American College Testing Program), as well as any specific college aid application forms—soon after January 1 of your child's senior year in hgh school, even before your child is accepted by a school. Once your child has been accepted, your child will receive an award letter from the school's financial aid office. This letter details how your child's eligibility for government aid was determined, how the need for college aid was calculated, and what kind and how much aid, if any, is being offered.

Your child doesn't necessarily have to jump at the first offer. If your child has been accepted by several schools, weigh the pros and cons of all the offers. If a school wants your child's enrollment badly enough, it might sweeten the initial offer. In the end, however, the financial aid package—while important —should not be the main deciding factor about which college your child finally enrolls in. Your child should believe that the academic and social offerings and the physical facilities will yield the best education you can afford.

▶ Working Your Way Across Country: Cooperative Education

By combining a full- or part-time job and a college career, your child can finance some or all of their education. The federal government sponsors thousands of students who take jobs in the armed forces, the Treasury Department, the Department of Health and Human Services, the Department of Agriculture, the General Services Administration, the Department of Justice, the Department of Labor, and many other agencies. Hundreds of private employers also offer co-op education opportunities.

The scheduling of work and school is flexible. Some students opt for parallel study and work, in which they attend school in the morning and work in the afternoon, or vice versa. The other option is to alternate semesters—one at work, then one at school.

Federal work-study. This program, available for both middle- and low-income students, allows your child to work a certain number of hours each week to earn a college grant and at least the minimum wage. Usually, your child works on campus in the cafeteria, library, or gym. In some cases, your child works for a local business in a field related to the course of study. Other jobs are offered at local, state, or federal public agencies. The program is administered by the college financial aid office, which sets the work schedule.

Your child cannot work more hours than the office approves and cannot earn more money than the work-study award.

For federal programs, pay is based on the civil service pay schedule. Federal work-study programs not only help students pay for schooling; they also expose students to real-world careers they would not experience in a classroom. To learn more about federal co-op education, contact the employment divisions of federal agencies directly or the Federal Job Information Center in Atlanta, Chicago, Dallas, Philadelphia, San Francisco, or Washington, D.C.

Americorps. The National Community Service Trust Act of 1993 established the Americorps program, in which students can finance some or all of their college education in return for agreeing to perform specified community service. Americorps volunteers receive a living stipend of about $7,500 a year and get the opportunity to accrue educational awards of $4,725 a year that can be used to pay tuition costs or repay student loans. Applicants must be U.S. citizens who are at least 17 and are high school graduates. Americorps volunteers typically work in underprivileged areas of American cities and rural districts in four fields: education, public safety, human services, and the environment. You can get all the details by contacting the Americorps Web site at http://www.americorps.org.

The Military. Your child's entire college tuition, plus a monthly allowance, will be paid if they attend one of the military academies, such as West Point for the U.S. Army, Annapolis for the U.S. Navy, or the Air Force Academy. Your child must then serve in the military for a specified number of years after graduation.

To get into these academies, however, your child must be nominated by your congressional representative or senator. Your child should apply to the academies during their junior year in high school. If the child would rather combine military training with education at a public or private university, they can apply to a Reserve Officer Training Corps (ROTC) program.

The U.S. Army and Air Force run their own ROTC programs, while the U.S. Navy and Marines operate a combined program. All ROTC programs offer both two-year and four-year terms. To enroll in ROTC, your child must be a high school graduate and be physically and academically qualified. After graduation and at least two years in the reserves, the child must serve at least four years of active duty in the service for which they were trained. ROTC programs also offer various specialty training courses, such as for doctors, nurses, and engineers. These programs can give your child a solid, marketable skill, making it easier to get a job once your child completes the military service. ROTC programs require that reservists attend both regular classes and ROTC courses while on campus. For more details about the ROTC, talk to a military recruiter.

▶ Fly Now, Pay Later: Borrowing for College

If the combination of savings, grants, scholarships, and work-study programs falls short of tuition costs, your child can apply for one of the many loans intended to finance college costs. Taking out a loan to finance college is a serious commitment that will probably take many years to repay, so help your child shop diligently for the best deal.

At the Crossroads: Sources of Loans

There are three main sources of loans: the federal or state government; colleges; and commercial enterprises such as banks or firms that specialize in college loans.

Route 1: Government loans

Several types of local and federal government loans exist. In this section we will take a look at Stafford, Perkins, and PLUS loans as well as state loans. So let's head off; there's a lot of territory to cover.

Stafford loans (formerly Guaranteed Student Loans): Stafford loans are available to all students, without regard to their financial status. Children of families that demonstrate need receive interest subsidies, while those considered less needy pay a higher interest rate. Your child can apply for a Stafford loan at financial institutions such as banks, savings and loans, credit unions, and state loan-guarantee agencies. Your child should apply as soon as the school accepts them because the application procedure and processing can take several months.

The Stafford program imposes certain limits on how much your child can borrow each year. Currently, a student may borrow

▶ $2,625 if the student is a first-year student enrolled in a program of study that is at least a full academic year,

▶ $3,500 if the student has completed a first year of study and the remainder of the program is at least a full academic year, and

▶ $5,500 if the student has completed two years of study and the remainder of the program is at least a full academic year.

If your child is an independent undergraduate student or a dependent student and you are unable to get a PLUS Loan (see below), the student may borrow annually up to

▶ $6,625 if the student is a first-year student enrolled in a program of study that is at least a full academic year (only $2,625 of this amount may be in subsidized loans),

▶ $7,500 if the student completed the first year of study and the remainder of the program is at least a full academic year (only $3,500 of this amount may be in subsidized loans), and

▶ $10,500 if the student has completed two years of study and the remainder of the program is at least a full academic year (only $5,500 of this amount may be in subsidized loans).

For periods of study that are less than an academic year, the amounts that may be borrowed will be less than those listed. Check with your school's financial aid office to find out how much your child may borrow. Stafford Loans are not made to students enrolled in programs that are less than one-third of an academic year.

Hazard!

Stafford Loans: Bumps In The Road

▶ These are the maximum yearly amounts you can borrow in both subsidized and unsubsidized loans. You might receive less than these amounts *if* you receive other financial aid that is used to cover a portion of your cost of attendance.

▶ Your school can refuse to certify your loan application or can certify a loan for an amount less than you would otherwise be eligible for *if* the school documents the reason for its action and explains the reason to you in writing. The school's decision is final and cannot be appealed to the U.S. Department of Education.

Generally, a graduate student can borrow up to $18,500 each academic year (only $8,500 of this amount may be in subsidized Stafford Loans).

Generally, the total debt you can have outstanding from all Stafford Loans combined is

- ▶ $23,000 as a dependent undergraduate student
- ▶ $46,000 as an independent undergraduate student (only $23,000 of this amount may be in subsidized loans)
- ▶ $138,500 as a graduate or professional student (only $65,500 of this amount may be in subsidized loans). The graduate debt limit includes any Stafford Loans received for undergraduate study.

Lenders of subsidized Stafford funds often charge a 5 percent loan origination fee, as well as an insurance fee of up to 3 percent, which are deducted from the loan proceeds. For unsubsidized Stafford loans, the combined origination and insurance fee might total 6.5 percent. Not all lenders charge the same fees, however; it pays to shop around.

Once a year, on June 30, the interest rate on Stafford loans is fixed at 3.1 percent more than the yield on a 91-day Treasury bill. By law, however, the rate cannot rise above 8.5 percent. If your child demonstrates financial need, the government will pay the interest on the loan while your child attends school, as well as for a six-month grace period after graduation.

If borrowing is not based on need, an unsubsidized Stafford loan accrues interest while your child attends school, though the repayment of the loan does not have to begin until after graduation. The minimum annual repayment amount on a single Stafford loan is $600, and your child can repay the loan in five to 10 years.

Perkins loans (formerly National Direct Student Loans): The college or university granting Perkins loans acts as the lender, using money provided by the federal government. These loans are designed for undergraduate and graduate students with *exceptional need*—meaning that their families earn $30,000 or less annually. Exceptional need is determined by the school's financial aid officer. Students can usually borrow up to $3,000 for each year of undergraduate study, up to a maximum of $15,000. Graduate students can usually borrow up to $5,000 a year, with total debt—including loans for undergraduate study—of no more than $30,000. If you go to a school with a default rate of under 7.5 percent, you can qualify for even more—$4,000 per undergraduate year up to $20,000 and $6,000 per graduate or professional year up to $40,000.

Perkins loans are extremely attractive for several reasons. First, they charge a flat 5 percent interest rate, which is lower than most other loans. Second, they allow a nine-month grace period following graduation before repayment must begin. Finally, the loans can be repaid over 10 years, which reduces the monthly payment considerably from shorter term student loan programs.

Parent Loans to Undergraduate Students (PLUS): PLUS loans are made to parents and are available through banks, savings and loans, credit unions, and some state lending agencies. PLUS loans allow parents to borrow an unlimited amount to finance college costs. However, PLUS loans and other financial aid cannot exceed the student's cost of attending school.

The interest rate of PLUS loans is set at 3.1 percent more than the one-year Treasury bill rate and is adjusted annually in June. The rate on PLUS loans cannot exceed 9 percent. Repayment of these loans must begin within 60 days of receiving the loan proceeds, and the loans can be repaid in five to 10 years.

Note: Many loans that formerly were processed through banks or other lending institutions are now granted directly through the Department of Education in the Federal Direct PLUS Program.

Working off your debt. In addition, thousands of students will be able to pay off their government loans through work in National Service Corporation.

Such work may include positions in state or local government, as well as in educational, environmental, law-enforcement, or social activities. Those entering the program could pay off as much as $5,000 worth of student loans for every year of service up to $10,000. For the latest information on all federal loan programs described here, call 800-4-FED-AID.

State loan programs. In addition to the federal aid, most states offer their own loan programs. Usually, these programs are designed for state residents; however, in some cases, even out-of-state students can qualify. The terms, interest rates, repayment schedules, and amounts of loans vary widely from state to state. Several states offer special incentive programs to train teachers, doctors, nurses, and other professionals in short supply. Other states offer programs aimed at veterans or those enlisted in the state's National Guard.

Route 2: College Loans

Most colleges, seeking to fill the gaps created by federal and state programs, offer their own loan programs. Rules vary widely, as some loans are designed for parents, others for students, and still others for both parents and students. Interest rates—usually tied to some index of Treasury securities —also range from very low to quite high, and repayment terms can be strict or lenient. Ask a school's financial aid officer about specific programs, preferably when your child applies to the school but certainly once the acceptance letter is in hand.

Route 3: Commercial Loans

In addition to the loans made by banks through government programs and as personal loans based on creditworthiness, several commercial lenders specialize in college lending. These programs allow your child to repay the principal on a loan after graduation, though the interest payments need to be made while still in school. Following are some of the major players in this market.

College Board. Its CollegeCredit program offers ExtraCredit loans to cover the full cost of your child's education. The minimum loan is $2,000. The loan's interest rate floats at 4½ percentage points over the 90-day Treasury bill rate, adjusted quarterly. There is a 3 percent loan-origination fee, and your child has 15 years to repay.

Another loan that is part of the CollegeCredit program is called the ExtraTime loan, which is designed to pay for a single year of education expenses. It has similar features to the ExtraCredit loan, except that you have the option of monthly payments of interest only while a student is enrolled, or monthly payments of principal and interest after the education is complete. For more information on these loans, call the College Board's College Answer Service line at 800-831-5626 or visit their Web site at http://www. collegeboard.com.

ConSern. ConSern Loans for Education lend up to $25,000 each year per child at the 30- or 90-day commercial paper rate plus 4.6 percentage points, adjusted monthly. ConSern charges a 4½ percent origination fee and allows your child to repay a loan over as long as 15 years. These loans are designed for employees of companies that have adopted the ConSern program. For more information on how to qualify, call ConSern at 800-767-5626 or go to http://www.consern.com.

The Education Resources Institute (TERI). TERI lends a minimum of $2,000 up to the cost of education minus financial aid per year per child at the prime rate plus 1½ to 2 percentage points, adjusted monthly with no cap. There are no fees and your child can repay in as much as 25 years. TERI also offers the Professional Education Plan (PEP) for graduate students. For more information, call TERI at 800-255-8374 or go to http://www.teri.com.

Key Education Resources. Key offers private supplemental loans such as the Key Alternative Loan, which allows undergraduates enrolled full-time to share the cost of their education. Key also offers the AchieverLoan to parents with three different ways to finance college or prep school tuitions. This loan charges 4½ percentage points over the 91-day Treasury bill rate, adjusted quarterly. Fees range from 3 percent to 5 percent of the loan amount, depending on the repayment method.

The Key CareerLoan is designed for adult students attending college part-time. Key also offers the Monthly Payment Plan, an interest-free budget plan administered through the school that allows families to make equal monthly payments to meet annual expenses. Key also offers several programs tailored to graduate students in specific fields such as law, business, medical, and dental schools. For more information, call Key at 800-KEY-LEND or visit http://www.key.com.

Nellie Mae. Formerly known as the New England Education Loan Marketing Association, Nellie Mae offers the EXCEL and SHARE programs, which will lend from $2,000 up to the cost of education minus the amount of other financial aid received by the student. The one-year renewable loans charge the prime rate plus 1.2 percent for the first year, plus an additional 1 percent in subsequent years; they are adjusted monthly. Nellie Mae charges a guarantee fee of 7 percent. You may repay both principal and interest on the loan or interest for up to four years while the student is still enrolled in school. Your child can repay the loan over as many as 20 years. For more information, call 800-367-8848 or visit the Nellie Mae Web site at http://www.nelliemae.com.

Sallie Mae (formerly the Student Loan Marketing Association). Sallie Mae, which buys and services federally insured educational loans made by lenders, has introduced several programs to reward borrowers who make on-time payments on their Stafford loans by reducing their interest rates.

▶ Great Rewards enables Stafford loan borrowers who make their first 48 scheduled monthly payments on time to receive an interest rate reduction of two full percentage points for the remaining term of the loan.

▶ SMART REWARDS is a similar program for SMART LOAN, which helps students consolidate their loans into one loan on advantageous terms. Borrowers who make their first 48 scheduled payments on time are rewarded with an interest rate reduction of one full percentage point for the remaining repayment term.

▶ The Great Returns Program helps heavily indebted Stafford borrowers who make their first 24 scheduled payments on time to receive an account credit equivalent to federal origination fees up to 3 percent (less $250).

▶ Direct Repay allows you to repay student loans through an automatic debit on your checking or savings account and earns you a quarter-point interest rate reduction on your loan as long as you make payments through the plan.

For more details on these programs, call the Sallie Mae Service Center at 800-524-9100 or the College Answer Service at 800-831-5626. You also can get more detail on these programs at Sallie Mae's Web site at http://www.salliemae.com.

The worksheet in Roadmap 6.2 summarizes the sources of assistance discussed in this chapter to give you an idea of the financial aid package you might expect for your child. It also lets you calculate the gap between that financial aid and what you still need to finance.

▶ Last Exit: Borrowing Against Your Assets

If the total financial aid package for which your child qualifies is not adequate, or if you want to cut down on outside borrowing, you might consider your last option: taking a loan against your assets. You may have accumulated substantial equity in certain assets that you can borrow against at a lower interest rate and with less hassle than your other borrowing options. The most obvious places to look for equity include the following:

Your Company Savings Plan. If you have participated in a salary reduction plan at work for several years, you probably have accumulated a substantial sum of money. Most employers will let you borrow against that money and

Roadmap 6.2

Financial Aid Package Worksheet

Item	$ Amount
1. **Costs of College** (tuition, room, board, fees)	$ _____
2. **Expected Family Contribution** (parents and students)	$ _____
3. **Financial Need** (subtract item 2 from item 1)	$ _____
4. **Sources of Aid**	
Grants and Scholarships	
Pell	$ _____
SEOG	_____
State	_____
College	_____
Private	_____
Work-Study	
Federal Work-Study	_____
ROTC or Other Military Aid	_____
Cooperative Education	_____
Loans	
Perkins	_____
Stafford (subsidized)	_____
Stafford (unsubsidized)	_____
PLUS/SLS	_____
State	_____
College	_____
Commercial	_____
Sources of Aid Total	$ _____
Gap Between Financial Need and Financial Aid (subtract item 4 from item 3)	$ _____

have you repay the loan through payroll deduction. Interest rates charged on such loans are often quite favorable at one or two percentage points more than the prime rate. However, borrow against your retirement savings only as a last resort. These plans are designed to provide long-term growth for your retirement years, not to pay college costs for your children.

While you're investigating options at your company, ask the employee benefits department whether your firm provides college loans or scholarships to children of employees. Some companies, particularly large corporations, offer such loans at attractive, below-market interest rates.

Traditional and Roth IRAs. A traditional IRA offers a tax deduction for contributions, and the funds may be used penalty-free for higher education. However, you're taxed on any withdrawals at your marginal income tax rate.

Your home. If you have paid down your mortgage and built up substantial equity in your home, you might be able to open a home-equity line of credit that charges only one to two percentage points more than the prime rate and allows you to repay it as quickly or as slowly as you wish, as long as you meet each month's minimum payment. An extra bonus is that all borrowing up to $100,000 is tax deductible. Remember, however, your home is on the line; if you default, the bank will foreclose. You can open a home-equity credit line with a bank, savings and loan, credit union, or mortgage company.

Your life insurance. With a permanent life insurance policy, you pay an annual premium to cover insurance expenses, plus an additional amount contributed to the cash value of the policy. The cash value grows tax-deferred. If you have amassed a large amount of cash value in the policy, you can usually borrow against it at a favorable interest rate to fund education expenses without owing any taxes. However, the amount you borrow from the policy reduces the death benefit, should you die before the loan is repaid. Again, consider this a last resort because such a loan will retard the growth of your cash value as well as lower your death benefit by the amount of the loan.

Taxable Accounts. A standard taxable account has the most flexibility when it comes to education savings. Account earnings are taxed, but if the earnings are the result of the sale of assets held for more than one year, they'll likely be subject to a lower capital gains rate of a maximum 20 percent (15 percent through 2008).

▶ Bonus Miles: Federal Tax Incentives for Education

There are several important incentives including federal tax deductions and tax credits. The amounts and rules differ with each incentive.

Mile 1: The Hope Scholarship Credit

Married taxpayers (filing jointly) with Adjusted Gross Income (AGI) of less than $85,000 and single taxpayers with AGI of less than $42,000 may claim the Hope Scholarship tax credit. There is a phase out of the credit for those with AGI of $85,000 to $105,000 for married taxpayers, $42,000 to $52,000 for single taxpayers (these numbers are periodically revised, so check when the time comes). The credit is not available to taxpayers with AGIs above those respective amounts.

The amount of the Hope Scholarship credit allowed is equal to 100 percent of qualified expenses (tuition and fees, but not room and board) up to $1,000 plus 50 percent of qualified expenses up to another $1,000, for a total maximum credit of $1,500 per student. The Hope credit only applies to students who are enrolled at least half-time and who have not completed their first two years of study. The credit cannot be claimed for more than two years for any one student.

Mile 2: Lifetime Learning Credit

Taxpayers can claim a Lifetime Learning Credit, subject to the same AGI limitations that apply to the Hope credit, for up to 20 percent of qualified expenses (tuition and fees) up to $10,000, for a total maximum credit of $2,000 per taxpayer.

If you have three children in college, your Hope credit may be as high as $4,500, but your Lifetime Learning Credit will never exceed $2,000 per year. Unlike with the Hope credit, the student doesn't have to be enrolled at least half-time, and there's no limit on the number of years the credit may be taken. However, you may not claim a Hope credit and a Lifetime Learning Credit for the same student in the same tax year. (These numbers are periodically revised, so check when the time comes.) See Roadmap 6.3 for a comparison of the two.

Both the Hope credit and the Lifetime Learning Credit belong to the person who claims the student as a dependent, even if someone else pays the expenses. If no one claims the student as a dependent, the student may claim the credit, even if someone else pays the expenses.

Roadmap 6.3

Comparison of Education Credits

Hope Credit	Lifetime Learning Credit
Up to $1,500 credit per eligible student	Up to $2,000 credit per *return*
Available ONLY until the first two years of post-secondary education are completed	Available for all years of postsecondary education and for courses to acquire or improve job skills
Available ONLY for two years per eligible student	Available for an unlimited number of years
Student must be pursuing an undergraduate degree or other recognized education credential	Student does not need to be pursuing a degree or other recognized education credential
Student must be enrolled at least half time for at least one academic period beginning during the year	Available for one or more courses
No felony drug conviction on student's record	Felony drug conviction rule does not apply

Mile 3: Tuition and Fees Deduction (Section 222) Deduction

As of this writing, a deduction for up to $4,000 of college tuition and related expenses is available for tax year for married taxpayers with AGI of less than $130,000 and for single taxpayers with AGI of less than $65,000. This is an above-the-line deduction, which means that you do not have to itemize your deductions to take advantage of this incentive. A deduction for up to $2,000 in college tuition and related expenses is available to married taxpayers with AGI as high as $160,000 and to single taxpayers with AGI as high as $80,000.

> *The Section 222 deduction is not available to taxpayers who claim a Hope or Lifetime Learning Credit for that student's expenses in the same tax year. You can choose the one that will give you the lower tax.*

You may be able to take a tuition and fees deduction for your education expenses instead of a Hope credit.

Mile 4: Student Loan Interest Deduction

Interest paid on student loans for undergraduate or graduate tuition, fees, books, and room and board may be deducted (above the line) by married taxpayers with AGI of less than $100,000 and by single taxpayers with AGI of less than $50,000. The deduction phases out for those married taxpayers with AGI of $100,000 to $130,000 and for single taxpayers with AGI of $50,000 to $65,000. The deduction is not available to taxpayers with AGI above those respective amounts. The deduction is to a maximum of $2,500 per year, with no limit on the number of years in which it's taken. The student must be enrolled at least half-time.

> *The Student Loan Interest Deduction is available to taxpayers who also claim a Hope or Lifetime Learning Credit. Students who are not claimed as a dependent may take the deduction on their own tax returns.*

▶ The Savvy Traveler: Other Tax Considerations

Generally, credits are more advantageous for taxpayers than deductions. Credits reduce the taxpayers' liability on a dollar-for-dollar basis, whereas a deduction only reduces the taxpayers' marginal income subject to taxation. Still, it pays to calculate the net tax benefit available under either a credit or a deduction before deciding which incentive to use.

If your AGI prevents a deduction or a credit, evaluate whether to give up your dependent's exemption so the student can claim an otherwise unavailable benefit. A qualified college financial planning advisor or your financial advisor or tax accountant can help you assess whether this approach makes sense for you.

Coverdell ESAs and Section 529 Plans. Distributions from a Coverdell ESA or a 529 Plan are tax-free if used for qualified higher education expenses. You may claim a Hope credit or a Lifetime Learning Credit and get the benefits of tax-free withdrawals from an Education Savings Account—all in the same year, on behalf of the same student. To determine whether any part of an ESA or a Section 529 Plan distribution is subject to taxation, qualified expenses must be reduced by the amount of any expenses used to generate a Hope or Lifetime Learning Credit.

For example, assume that you incur $10,000 in qualified expenses and take a distribution from a 529 Plan to cover those expenses. If you claim the $2,000 Lifetime Learning Credit ($10,000 × 20 percent), you must reduce your Education Funding qualified expenses by $10,000, leaving no qualified expenses to apply to the 529 distribution. As a result, a portion of your distribution may be subject to both income tax and a 10 percent federal tax penalty.

▶ Traveling Online: Using Your Computer to Finance a College Education

The computer can make the search for financial aid much more efficient and productive than the old-fashioned way of wading through books and filling out applications and financial aid forms by hand. There are enormous resources available through the Internet to help you calculate how much financial aid you need and help you find as much as possible.

Many of the Web sites listed in Appendix B contain calculators that help you figure out how much colleges will expect parents to pay, how much will be provided in financial aid, depending on the parent's financial circumstances, and what kind of loan repayment schedule you can expect. Other Web sites contain mountains of information on scholarships, grants, and loans that your child may be able to qualify for. There are also several CD-ROMs allowing you to search for scholarships that your child might have a good chance of getting—these disks often are sold along with scholarship listing books.

Most colleges and universities also have elaborate Web sites allowing you to take a "virtual tour" of their campus and find out about course offerings and the amount of financial aid available. It is certainly a lot cheaper and less time consuming to tour several campuses online than it is to go there in person. You also can fill out applications for college, as well as financial aid forms, and submit them electronically. This can save your child a great deal of time and effort retyping the forms many times.

We have included a representative sample of the Web sites on the Internet in Appendix B to help you understand the entire financial aid process. Using these resources can potentially save you thousands of dollars in college costs, so they are definitely worth investigating.

Whether you assemble the money to pay for your children's college education from savings and investments, grants, scholarships, and/or loans, the costs are burdensome.

The earlier you develop a plan to fund college, the easier you will handle this burden.

Appendix A

An Itinerary

Here's a quick review of what to do, as you set out on the road to saving for college.

Stop #1. Before you can begin saving and investing for your child's education, you need to determine what your other goals are and understand how saving for a college education for your child fits in with your other needs and goals.

- ▶ College financing is a process, not a product. It involves seeking advice, reviewing options, and creating a plan for ensuring that your assets are sufficient to meet your goals.
- ▶ Setting specific financial objectives and putting them in writing—listing dollar amounts and noting exactly when you will need the money—will motivate you to achieve your goals—whatever they may be.
- ▶ Saving for college is a medium to long-term goal for most people; it is also a family affair. If you are married or living with a partner, make certain that your goals—including saving for college educations for the kids—is a goal to which both of you are committed.
- ▶ Roadmaps 1.1 to 1.3 will help you focus on what your short-, medium-, and long-term goals are. Roadmap 1.4 will help you put each of these goals in perspective and set priorities and understand timeframes and the costs of each of these goals. Roadmap 1.5 will help you track how well you're doing at meeting your goals.
- ▶ Using this information will help you determine how to achieve them. What are you willing to do to make your goal a reality? Will it involve working overtime or finding a second job? Will it mean tradeoffs—cutting back or eliminating expenses such as movies, meals out, or a new car every three years? How much will you have to save each week, month, or year to reach your goals?
- ▶ Other important questions to ask yourself are: How much of my child's college education do I want to pay for—all, part, undergraduate, graduate, public or private college? Should my child work to pay for some of the schooling? Should they/we take out loans to pay for schooling? Should I

put away money for that education if it means not saving for retirement? The answers to these questions will affect how much money you need to save for educating your child.

▶ Once you know how much you will need, you must determine how much time you have to save/invest to reach that goal. Roadmaps 1.5 and 1.6 will take you through that process and Roadmap 1.7 will show you what your present income is and where it's going. That will give you a handle on the current state of affairs and lead you along the road to creating a budget (Roadmap 1.8) that will allow you to reach this very important new goal, without losing sight of your other goals.

▶ By the way, have you noticed how the process of working your way through each of these roadmaps has helped you define and refine your other goals? That's a side benefit of financial travel: You get to focus on what's really important.

Stop #2: Just deciding that you want to fund a child's education is an important first step. It's now important to assess how you are going to make it happen in light of where you are now, both in terms of your present finances and your time horizon.

▶ The first step is to refine what was an educated guess at the cost of a college education. Now it's time to determine how much money you're *really* going to need.

▶ It's now time to figure out what kind of jumpstart, if any, you have toward that goal. To do that you must determine your *net worth*. Roadmaps 2.1 and 2.2 will get you there by totting up your total assets and liabilities. Doing this exercise will also give you a bird's eye view of the terrain and allow you to figure out just how far along the road you are.

▶ Roadmap 2.3 will help you estimate college costs at the time your child is ready to enroll and how much you need to save. Take a deep breath and don't panic; very few families actually save the full amount needed to pay for college. Colleges generally expect that you will save about one-third of the required amount, borrow one-third, and fund another third from your cash flow while your child is in college. You need to know how to maximize your savings in keeping with your risk tolerance and timeframe.

Stop #3: The higher the return you earn on your savings and investments, the less money you must set aside for your children's college tuition.

Unfortunately, because no guarantees of high returns exist in the investment world without commensurate high risks, you should put together a balanced portfolio of high-, medium-, and low-risk investments to fund your children's college.

- ▶ The first thing you're going to do at this stop is determine your own unique tolerance for risk. To do this, you must understand the many risk factors that can affect the way you save and invest, including the risk of not taking any risk.
- ▶ Once you've understood where you stand in terms of your risk tolerance and how that aligns with your time horizon, it's time to take a look at different types of investments to see how they align with your time horizon and your risk tolerance. This will help you assemble a portfolio that achieves your financial goals and still allows you to sleep comfortably at night. Roadmap 3.1 will help you visualize an entire mix of assets and where they fit.
- ▶ Having understood risk and where different investments generally fall, it's time to think about allocating your assets—you need to decide how you allocate your resources in your investment portfolio. It all boils down to how much you want to put in stocks, real estate, bonds, cash, and so on. As you now know, much of this depends on your unique circumstances like age, time horizon, your other financial goals, and tolerance for investment risk as well as external factors. Reminder: Asset allocation is not a one-time event; as circumstances change, your portfolio's asset mix will change over time, too.
- ▶ Exploring and understanding the major types of investments—stocks, bonds, and mutual funds—is essential to the wise investor. Hot tips, like the lottery, may be winners for some few lucky speculators, but when you are saving for something as important as a college education for your children, it takes a lot more than luck. Before you invest, make certain you understand the various types of investments—not every stock, bond, or mutual fund is alike!
- ▶ Remember, saving and investing for college doesn't mean forgetting the rest of your goals. Apply this knowledge to your other goals. It will help you achieve some of the other things you work so hard for.

Stop #4: Now that you have an understanding of the various types of investments available to you, there's another very important decision you should consider: Are you prepared to take on the work of doing it yourself or do you want to work with a financial advisor? Whatever the answer to this question, you are the one ultimately responsible, and you'll have to decide where exactly you are going to invest your college funds.

▶ To determine whether or not to work with a financial advisor, ask yourself: (1) Do I know everything I need to know about asset allocation college funding vehicles, tax-reduction strategies, and financial aid? (2) Do I want to invest the time and effort to learn these issues? (3) Do I want to continue to invest the time it takes to keep up with the markets and remain competent as an investor? If you answered yes to these questions and have the time and interest to devote yourself to building and protecting your assets, then you can go it alone.

▶ For those who answered "no," it's time to find an advisor. Those who answered "yes" may still want to find an advisor, if only for some parts of their analysis, strategizing, or investing. For example, if, as you do, you have a specific long-term goal, such as saving enough to fund your children's college education and build a retirement nest egg, a financial planner can start you on the right path.

▶ If you are hiring a financial advisor, it's important to know what to look for, what to ask, and how to assess a planner. It's also important to know what services you should reasonably expect and the various ways in which planners get paid.

▶ Prepare carefully for your first meeting with a planner. First impressions do make a difference, and it is of the utmost importance that you feel at ease with the advisor from the very start. Money is a very personal and private matter. Come prepared with any pertinent financial documents and a list of questions and concerns.

▶ The best long-term strategy is to diversify among investment assets and styles. If half your holdings are in growth stocks and the other half are in value stocks, you will perform better over time than if you invest all your money in one style of stock.

▶ As a strategy for building a college fund, fixed-income securities provide much more current income than stocks but much less growth potential. Invest a smaller amount of your assets, perhaps 30 percent, in them while your child is young. When your child becomes a teenager, put more money in fixed-income investments, which have less risk of falling sharply in value than do stocks.

► Before you decide to invest in individual stocks and/or bonds—especially if you are planning to fly solo—take a good look at mutual funds. They offer several key advantages over owning individual stocks and/or bonds for all investors, but especially the novice investor and the investor with limited funds.

► In the end you must decide if investing in mutual funds or in individual stocks, bonds, or a combination of all three is right for you. There are advantages and disadvantages to both and several things, like taxes and the types of accounts in which your investments are held, that may affect your decision.

► At least once a year, measure the returns on your portfolio against those of the index that most accurately reflects its components. If the performance is as good as or better than the benchmark, you are on track. If the performance falls short of the benchmark, consider changing the investments that correspond to that asset class.

► As you invest, never forget the nine common money management mistakes that are all too easy to make.

Stop #5: Now, you must decide where to park your child's college fund and in whose name the money should be held. Just as there are many ways to invest for college, there are also a number of different types of accounts available to you. Each has pluses and minuses and each is designed to fit the needs of different families and different financial situations.

► Custodial Accounts: UGMA/UTMA accounts may be set up to transfer assets to minors without incurring gift taxes or filing gift-tax returns (assuming you stay under the annual gift exclusion). For some, these accounts are better for reducing the size of an estate than saving for college. UGMA/UTMA accounts can hurt financial aid eligibility and are taxed at a parent's tax rate until the child reaches age 14. If you have the money, a simpler approach may be to pay the student's tuition directly to the college. Such payments are excluded from the gift documentation and tax provisions and are not limited in amount.

► Series EE and Series I Bonds may appeal to families that expect to meet the income limitations at redemption, have a low risk tolerance and short time horizon, and, therefore, are willing to accept the relatively low returns.

► Coverdell Education Savings Account (ESA) allows you to deposit $2,000 per year per child under age 18 into an account on a tax-deferred basis.

However, your current income affects both the degree and whether or not you can participate in or benefit from an ESA. If your income falls above the range, you cannot make a contribution at all; however, another individual whose income is not too high—like a grandparent, friend, or even the child—may contribute. An ESA is definitely worth considering, even if it's just one of the ways in which you save, and, if you have a child with special needs, the law has a number of unique provisions designed especially for them.

▶ Qualified tuition plans, also known as 529 Plans, are a popular education savings method that feature special tax benefits and allow significantly greater contributions than other options like the Coverdell Education Savings Account. Every state and the District of Columbia now has at least one 529 Plan. Anyone—parents, relatives, and friends—can contribute money to a 529 Plan on behalf of a beneficiary (student), and, unlike Coverdell ESAs, contributors are not subject to income limitations, nor are there restrictions on the beneficiary's age. Prepaid plans are considered a student resource and result in a dollar-for-dollar reduction in financial aid. However, 529 Savings Plans are considered the owner's asset, not the beneficiary's. If the owner is the parent, up to 6 percent of the account's value will be included in the financial aid formulas. However, any dollar amount spent from the plan for your child's education will be considered the student's income. In general, 529 Plans tend to be most appropriate for families who do not expect to qualify for financial aid or who do not want to count on financial aid.

▶ Life insurance cash values generally are not assessed in the financial aid calculation, but liquid savings are. Moreover, withdrawals from the VUL (to pay for tuition, for example) are not treated as income, thereby lowering total assessable income in the years during which the student is attending college and applying for aid. For this reason, saving through Variable Universal Life Insurance may be valuable, but if you don't need life insurance this is probably not the vehicle for you as there are many downsides as well.

▶ Whose name is on the account can have great consequences in terms of taxes and financial aid and, if your adult child decides to squander the money instead of paying for college, it's out of your control. Explore each option carefully before deciding who owns which, if any, account.

▶ For many people, education is an important aspect of life. Parents want to see their children get an education, and grandparents want to ensure that their grandchildren get an education. Should you die when your children or grandchildren are very young or before they finish their education, the provisions you include in your estate plan can make all the difference to them, so consider them very carefully.

Stop #6: Even if you have saved diligently and amassed a large college fund —and particularly if you haven't been so conscientious—you will likely need to apply for financial aid to cover at least part of your children's college costs. Many grants, loans, scholarships, and other programs exist, some offering better opportunities than others, including need- and merit-based aid, private financial aid, and tuition discounts. Obviously, not everyone will qualify for each of these, but, before rejecting any of them, it's important to investigate each type.

Sources for grants and scholarships include:

▶ Pell Grants, which are given mostly to students in low-income families. Amounts vary based on funding grant, and the cost of tuition, whether student is full- or part-time, and attending for a full academic year. Your child should apply even if you know that it is difficult to get one, because colleges normally won't consider a student for another grant unless they have been rejected for a Pell.

▶ Supplemental educational opportunity grants, which go to undergraduates, range from $100 to $4,000 a year, with larger amounts of money going to lower income students. The priority goes to those receiving Pell grants.

▶ State programs for residents. These vary widely—your child's high school guidance counselor should know the details of grants available in your state.

▶ Most institutions offer several kinds of grants, which may or may not be based on financial need; for information contact the school's financial aid office.

▶ Thousands of private grants and scholarship programs are available to students with superior academic records, special interests, and other qualifying characteristics. Some of them may surprise you; investigate these sources carefully, and beware of scams.

▶ Financial Aid. To receive financial aid, a student must prove that the family needs the money. To determine how much, a standard *needs analysis* examines what the parents can afford to pay and what the student can contribute. Financial aid is designed to supplement, not replace, a family's contribution to college costs. Therefore, all lenders expect a family to pay as much as possible. Public and private schools use the FAFSA to allocate federal aid. Private colleges often require the PROFILE (and sometimes their own form) to determine how money is allocated. To apply for financial aid, you must complete these forms in January and February of your child's senior year of high school—and then every year while the child is in college. Roadmap 6.2 will help you navigate the process and estimate what you need and how much you can expect in financial aid.

▶ Work-Study and Co-op Education programs. By combining a full- or part-time job and a college career, your child can finance some or all of their education. The federal government sponsors thousands of students as does the military and Americorps. In addition, hundreds of private employers also offer co-op education opportunities.

▶ Borrowing for College. If the combination of savings, grants, scholarships, and work-study programs falls short of tuition costs, your child can apply for one of the many loans intended to finance college costs. Taking out a loan to finance college is a serious commitment that will probably take many years to repay, so help your child shop diligently for the best deal. Sources of loans include state and federal government, colleges, commercial lending institutions, and borrowing against your assets. Some forms of borrowing are more advantageous from a tax and interest point of view, so examine all options carefully before making a decision.

▶ The Internet can make the search for financial aid much more efficient and productive than the old-fashioned way of wading through books and filling out applications and financial aid forms by hand. There are enormous resources available through the Internet to help you calculate how much financial aid you need and help you find as much as possible.

Over a working lifetime, the College Board estimates that the typical college graduate earns, on average, over $1 million more than a high school graduate does. If you add a graduate degree, the difference is even greater (as much as $2 million more). It's no wonder that most parents want to help provide a college education for their children!

The earlier you develop a plan to fund college, the easier the trip will be. *Bon voyage!*

Appendix B

The Best of *Saving/Paying for College*: A Resource Guide

► Bibliography

The following books were used as resources for this book. In addition, we have provided lists of other books and Web sites that offer more detailed information on some of the topics covered in this book. We hope you find all these resources useful.

Anthony, Mitch. *The New Retirementality*. Chicago: Dearborn Trade Publishing, 2001.

Barney, Coleen Esq. and Victoria Collins, Ph.D., CFP. *Best Intentions*. Chicago: Dearborn Trade Publishing, 2002.

Downing, Neil. *The New IRAs and How to Make Them Work for You*. Chicago: Dearborn Trade Publishing, 2002.

Garrett, Sheryl. *Just Give Me the Answers: Expert Advisors Address Your Most Pressing Financial Questions*. Chicago: Dearborn Trade Publishing, 2004.

Goodman, Jordan E. *Everyone's Money Book,* 3rd ed. Chicago: Dearborn Trade Publishing, 2001.

Lawrence, Judy. *The Budget Kit,* 4th ed. Chicago: Dearborn Trade Publishing, 2004.

Lewis, Allyson, CFP. *The Million Dollar Car and $250,000 Pizza*. Chicago: Dearborn Trade Publishing, 2000.

▶ Recommended Books and Web Sites

For Chapters 1 and 2, Defining Your Financial Goals and Funding a College Education
Web Sites

A wealth of financial planning information is easily accessible via the Internet. The quality of information varies; many commercial sites focus on product sales pitches and provide little useful information; others provide objective, unbiased information.

Savingforcollege.com. offers information on college funding, with access to a college savings calculator and a nationwide college tuition database. Many consider this the best Web site on the subject of college funding. http://www.savingforcollege.com.

For Chapters 3 and 4, ABCs of Investing for College and What You Need to Know Before You Invest
Books

General Investor's Guides

▶ *The Complete Idiot's Guide to Online Investing* by Douglas Gerlach. Penguin Group USA, Penguin Group (USA) Inc., 405 Murray Hill Parkway, East Rutherford, NJ 07073. Telephone: 800-788-6262 (http://www.penguinputnam.com). An easy-to-understand guide to the basics of investing, researching options, and using the Internet for portfolio management.

▶ *The Finance and Investment Handbook,* 6th ed., by John Downes and Jordan E. Goodman. Barron's Educational Series, 250 Wireless Blvd., Hauppauge, NY 11788. Telephone: 631-434-3311; 800-645-3476 (http://www.barronseduc.com). Everything you need to know about finance and investing; explains investment alternatives, how to read the financial pages of newspapers and annual reports; includes a dictionary of 5,000 terms; and lists of stocks, mutual funds, futures and options, currencies, and more.

▶ *The First Time Investor: How to Start Safe, Invest Smart & Sleep Well,* 3rd ed., by Larry Chambers. The McGraw-Hill Companies, P.O. Box 182604, Columbus, OH 43272. Telephone: 877-833-5524 (http://www.mcgraw-hill.com). Packed with easy-to-use information on every aspect of investing.

▶ *Getting Started in Stocks* by Alvin Hall. John Wiley & Sons, 10475 Crosspoint Blvd. Indianapolis, IN 46256. Telephone: 877-762-2974 (http://www.wiley.com). A primer on the basics of stock investing.

▶ *How to Invest $50–$5,000: The Small Investor's Step-by-Step, Dollar-by-Dollar Plan for Low-Risk, High-Value Investing,* 8th ed., by Nancy Dunnan. HarperBusiness, P.O.Box 588, Dunmore, PA 18512. Telephone: 212-207-7000; 800-331-3761 (http://www.harpercollins.com). Written with the beginning investor in mind; covers the full range of personal finance investment.

▶ *Investing Online for Dummies,* 4th ed., by Kathleen Sindell. John Wiley & Sons, 10475 Crosspoint Blvd., Indianapolis, IN 46256. Telephone: 877-762-2974 (http://www.dummies.com). Covers all the basics for the on-line investor, including setting up stock screens, selecting mutual funds, looking for IPOs, and online banking and trading.

▶ *The Neatest Little Guide to Stock Market Investing,* Revised edition by Jason Kelly. Penguin-Putnam, 405 Murray Hill Parkway, East Rutherford, NJ 07073. Telephone: 800-788-6262 (http://www. penguinputnam. com). Provides friendly guidance, sound financial expertise, and all the information needed to make smart stock choices.

▶ *The 100 Best Stocks to Own for Under $25,* by Gene Walden. Dearborn Trade, 30 S. Wacker Dr., Chicago, IL 60606. Telephone: 312-836-4400; 800-245-2665 (http://www.dearborntrade.com).

▶ *One Up on Wall Street,* by Peter Lynch. Simon & Schuster, Simon & Schuster Mail Order, 100 Front Street, Riverside, NJ 08075. Telephone: 800-323-7445 (http://www.simonandschuster.com). A compendium of sensible advice from the former manager of Fidelity's legendary Magellan Fund.

▶ *The Only Investment Guide You Will Ever Need,* expanded and updated edition by Andrew Tobias. Harcourt, 15 East 26th Street, New York, NY, 10010. Telephone: 212-592-1000. This classic, easy-to-read book covers many of the basics of personal finance, from investments and life insurance to Social Security.

▶ *A Random Walk Down Wall Street:* completely revised and updated eighth edition, by Burton G. Malkiel. W.W. Norton & Co., Inc., 500 Fifth Ave., New York, NY 10110. Telephone: 212-354-5500 (http://www.wwnorton. com). This updated investment classic is a comprehensive guide to the market. Also provides a life-cycle guide to investing.

▶ *Security Analysis: Principles and Techniques,* 3rd ed., by Benjamin Graham and David Dodd. The McGraw-Hill Companies, P.O. Box 182604, Columbus, OH 43272. Telephone: 877-833-5524 (http://www.mcgraw-hill.com). Written by the fathers of fundamental stock analysis, this book is their seminal work on the subject.

▶ *Value Investing Today,* 3rd ed., by Charles Brandes. The McGraw-Hill Companies, P.O. Box 182604, Columbus, OH 43272. Telephone: 877-833-5524 (http://www.mcgraw-hill.com). International look at value investment approach from one of its most famed practitioners.

▶ *What You Need to Know Before You Invest: An Introduction to the Stock Market and Other Investments,* 3rd ed., by Rod Davis. Barron's Educational Series, 250 Wireless Blvd., Hauppage, NY 11788. Telephone: 516-434-3311; 800-645-3476 (http://www.barronseduc.com). Explains the stock market, how it works, and the Dow. Advises how to select a broker, open a brokerage account, invest in bonds and mutual funds, and how to read financial statements.

Mutual Funds

▶ *Bogle on Mutual Funds: New Perspectives for the Intelligent Investor* by John Bogle. Dell, 1745 Broadway, New York, NY 10036. Telephone: 212-782-9000. The founder and chairman of the Vanguard mutual funds group gives advice on setting up a portfolio of funds to meet investment objectives, spotting excessive fees and false advertising claims, and interpreting mutual fund data.

▶ *Mutual Funds for Dummies,* 3rd ed., by Eric Tyson and James C. Collins. John Wiley & Sons, 10475 Crosspoint Blvd., Indianapolis, IN 46256. Telephone: 877-762-2974; http://www.dummies.com. Simplifies financial planning and points to the mutual fund investments best suited for you.

Financial Advisors

▶ *The Right Way to Hire Financial Help: A Complete Guide to Choosing and Managing Brokers, Financial Planners, Insurance Agents, Lawyers, Tax Preparers,* 2nd ed., by Charles A. Jaffe. The MIT Press, c/o Triliteral, 100 Maple Ridge Drive, Cumberland, RI 02864. Telephone: 617-625-8569; 800-405-1619 (http://www.mitpress.mit.edu). Takes readers through the basics of hiring and managing financial professionals. Offers specific questions to determine if the person is a good qualified match to your needs.

Magazines

Weekly and monthly investment magazines usually give far more detail on individual stocks than do newspapers.

- ▶ *Forbes* (60 Fifth Ave., New York, NY 10011. Telephone: 212-620-2200; 800-888-9896; http://www.forbes.com). Uncovers good stocks and exposes stocks it considers overpriced.
- ▶ *Fortune* (1271 Avenue of the Americas, New York, NY 10020. Telephone: 212-522-1212; 800-541-1000; http://www.fortune.com). A business magazine with extensive coverage of Wall Street and stock selection. *Fortune* also publishes an annual Investor's Guide offering many stock ideas.
- ▶ *Money* (Time and Life Building, Rockefeller Center, New York, NY 10020. Telephone: 212-522-1212; 800-541-1000; http://www.pathfinder.com/money). Publishes several articles each month on individual stocks and mutual funds, as well all other areas of personal finance, including banking, taxes, real estate, and financing college education.
- ▶ *SmartMoney* (1755 Broadway, 2nd Floor, New York, NY 10019. Telephone: 800-444-4204; http://www.smartmoney.com). This personal business magazine features practical ideas for investing, spending, and saving.
- ▶ *Kiplinger's Personal* (Kiplinger Washington Editors Inc., 1729 H Street NW, Washington, DC 20006. Telephone: 800-544-0155; http://www.kiplinger.com). Finance reports on investments, taxes, insurance, paying for college, planning for retirement, home ownership, major purchases such as cars and computers, and other personal finance topics.

Trade Associations

- ▶ American Institute of Certified Public Accountants (1211 Avenue of the Americas, New York, NY 10036-8775. Telephone: 212-596-6200; 888-777-7077; http://www.aicpa.org). Can help you find a tax-oriented accountant or one who provides financial planning services. Also licenses Personal Financial Specialists (PFS), who are accountants concentrating on financial planning. For a list of PFS members nationally, call 888-999-9256. Will send a copy of the following brochures: "How to Choose and Use a CPA" and "Invest in Your Future: Choose a Personal Financial Specialist."

▶ American Society of CLU & ChFC (270 S. Bryn Mawr Ave., Bryn Mawr, PA 19010-2195. Telephone: 610-526-2500; 888-243-2258; http://www.the americancollege.edu). The association of insurance and financial services professionals holding the Chartered Life Underwriters (CLU) and Chartered Financial Consultants (ChFC) designations will refer you to an insurance agent or a financial consultant in your area; will also send a free copy of "How to Select a Qualified Financial Consultant."

▶ CFA Institute (560 Ray C. Hunt Dr., Charlottesville, VA 22903-0668. Telephone: 804-951-5499; 800-247-8132; http://www.aimr.org). Confers the Chartered Financial Analyst (CFA) designation on those who have passed a series of examinations relating to investment management. The Association offers a series of free investor fact sheets on "How to Evaluate Portfolio Performance," "How to Select an Investment Advisor," "Defining Your Investment Objectives," and "Managing the Relationship Between You and Your Advisor."

▶ Certified Financial Planner Board of Standards (1700 Broadway, Suite 2100, Denver, CO 80290. Telephone: 303-830-7500; 888-237-6275; http://www.cfp-board.org). Administers CFP examinations and licenses individuals to use the CFP designation. Contact the CFP Board to check if a planner is certified, if they have been disciplined by the Board, or to lodge a complaint. For referrals to financial planners in your area, contact the International Association for Financial Planning or the Institute of Certified Financial Planners.

▶ The Financial Planning Association (3801 E. Florida Ave., Suite 708, Denver, CO 80210. Telephone: 303-759-4900; 800-322-4237; http://www.fpanet.org). Represents financial planners who have passed the CFP examination; will refer you to three planners in your area; also publishes *The Journal of Financial Planning,* and will send free copies of the following: "The CFP Professional," "Q and A about Financial Planning," and "Selecting a Qualified Financial Planning Professional: Twelve Questions to Consider." On the Institute's Web site is a publication titled "Your Children's College Bill: How to Figure It . . . How to Pay for It."

▶ The Garrett Planning Network, Inc. (Telephone: 866-260-8400; http://www.garrettplanningnetwork.com) is an international network of independent financial advisors and planners offering hourly as-needed financial planning and advice to anyone regardless of income.

▶ Institute of Business and Finance (7911 Herschel Ave., Suite 201, La Jolla, CA 92037. Telephone: 800-848-2029; 858-454-4073; http://www.icfs.com). Organization granting the Certified Fund Specialist (CFS) designation; also sponsors several other board-certified designations in other areas of personal finance, including estate planning, securities, insurance, income taxes, mutual funds, and financial planning.

▶ Investment Counsel Association of America (1050 17th St., Suite 725, Washington, DC 20036. Telephone: 202-293-4222; http://www.icaa.org). Professional organization of independent investment counsel firms that manage the assets of individuals, pension plans, trusts, and nonprofit institutions such as foundations. Offers a free membership directory for those looking for an investment counselor.

▶ National Association of Professional Financial Advisors (NAPFA) (3250 North Arlington Heights Road, Suite 109, Arlington Heights, IL 60004. Telephone: 800-366-2732 or 847-483-5400; http://www.napfa. org). NAPFA's mission is to provide consumers of all income levels with fee-only comprehensive financial advice including retirement, saving for college, insurance, estates, taxes, selling your business, and many more financial issues.

U.S. Government Regulator

▶ Federal Trade Commission (6th St. and Pennsylvania Ave., N.W., Washington, D.C. 20580. Telephone: 202-326-2222; 877-FTC-HELP; http://www.ftc.gov). Offers many helpful brochures, including "Facts about Financial Planners" and "How to Talk To and Select Lawyers, Financial Planners, Tax Preparers and Real Estate Brokers." It lists FTC publications, Consumer Alerts, Education Campaigns, and the Consumer's Action Handbook, and allows you to lodge fraud complaints.

For Chapters 5 and 6, Savings and Investment Vehicles, Financial Aid, and Other Sources of Money
Books

▶ *College Money Handbook.* Peterson's Publishing, Princeton Pike Corporate Center, 2000 Lenox Dr., P.O. Box 67005, Lawrenceville, NJ 08648. Telephone: 800-643-5506 (http://www.petersons.com). Profiles hundreds of colleges and what financial aid they have to offer; includes a CD-ROM to help you estimate college costs.

► *The Fiske Guide to Colleges* by Edward B. Fiske. Sourcebooks, Inc., 1935 Brookdale Rd., Suite 139, Naperville, IL 60563. Telephone: 800-43-BRIGHT, 630-961-3900 (http://www.sourcebooks.com). The most frequently asked questions about attending college, from academics to social life; includes a section on getting a first-rate education at public university prices.

► *Paying for College: Without Going Broke,* by Kalman A. Chany and Geoff Martz. Princeton Review, 2315 Broadway, New York, NY 10024. Telephone: 800-2-REVIEW (http://www.princetonreview.com). Helps you plan ahead to improve your child's chances of getting financial aid, calculate aid eligibility before applying to colleges, complete financial aid forms, negotiate with financial aid offices, and learn about educational tax breaks.

► *The Scholarship Book,* revised and updated, by Daniel J. Cassidy, Founding Editor, revised by Ellen Schneid Coleman Research Group. Prentice Hall Press/Penguin Group USA, Penguin Group (USA) Inc., 405 Murray Hill Parkway, East Rutherford, NJ 07073. Telephone: 800-788-6262. The ultimate listing of private sector scholarships, loans, and grants; includes searchable CD-ROM.

► *Scholarships, Grants & Prizes.* Peterson's Publishing, Princeton Pike Corporate Center, 2000 Lennox Dr., P.O. Box 67005, Lawrenceville, NJ 08648. Telephone: 800-643-5506 (http://www. petersons.com). Extensive listings of scholarships, including searchable CD-ROM.

Trade Associations and Companies Specializing In College Financing

► ACT Inc. (formerly American College Testing). 500 ACT Drive, P.O. Box 168, Iowa City, Iowa 52243-0168. Telephone: 319-337-1270; http://www.act.org. Administers tests and advises financial aid administrators and students; processes the Free Application for Federal Student Aid (FAFSA).

► The College Board. 45 Columbus Ave., New York, NY 10023-6992. Telephone: 212-713-8000 (http://www.collegeboard.org). Publishes many books and CD-ROMs on financing college; sponsors a loan program called CollegeCredit® (call 800-927-4302 for more information). The Board's College Scholarship Service administers the CSS/Financial Aid

PROFILE program, used by many colleges to help determine a student's need for financial aid.

▶ College Savings Bank. 5 Vaughn Dr., Princeton, NJ 08540-6313. Telephone: 800-888-2723 (http://www.collegesavings.com). Sells the CollegeSure® CD, designed to let parents prepay college education costs, either in a lump sum or in smaller amounts over time. CD pays a variable rate indexed to the change in college costs.

▶ ConSern. 205 Van Buren St., Suite 200, Herndon, VA 20170. Telephone: 703-709-5626; 800-767-5624 (http://www.consern.com). Sponsors the ConSern Loans for Education program, through which about 5,000 employers offer education loans for either undergraduate or graduate study to their employees at advantageous rates. Loan proceeds can be used.

▶ TERI—The Education Resources Institute. 31 St. James Ave., 6th Floor, Boston, MA 02116. Telephone: 800-255-8374 (http://www.teri.org). Offers loans based on creditworthiness, not income limitations or need; offers a variety of free brochures describing their loan program.

▶ Key Education Resources. 745 Atlantic Ave., Suite 300, Boston, MA 02111-2735; Telephone: 617-348-0010; 800-KEY-LEND (http://www.keybank.com/educate.htm). Provides federal and private financing options, payment plans, and counseling from prep school through graduate school; Web site features KeyScape, a software program allowing you to calculate your estimated family contribution and project a typical budget for repaying loans once you have graduated, among other features; you can also apply for a loan online.

▶ National Commission for Cooperative Education. 360 Huntington Ave., Boston, MA 02115. Telephone: 617-373-3778 (http://www.co-op.edu/). Ask for a free copy of *Cooperative Education Undergraduate Program Directory.*

▶ The National Association of State Treasurers. (P.O. Box 11910, Lexington, KY 40578-1910. Telephone: 606-244-8175; 877-277-6496 (http://www.collegesavings.org). College Savings Plans Network includes information about state-sponsored college savings plans and prepaid tuition plans, plus links to various states' plans: http://www.collegesavings.org.

▶ Nellie Mae. 50 Braintree Hill Office Park, Suite 300, Braintree, MA 02184. Telephone: 800-634-9308; 781-849-1325 (http://www.nelliemae.com). Offers the EXCEL and SHARE student loan programs for undergraduate or graduate study as well as a loan consolidation program, allowing you to consolidate several student loans into one manageable payment. Nellie Mae offers two free brochures explaining the college financing process: "Get Ready for College" is designed for parents with children in elementary or junior high school; "Steps to Success" is aimed at those with high school-age children.

▶ Sallie Mae. 11600 Sallie Mae Dr., Reston, VA 20193. Telephone: 703-810-3000 (http://www.salliemae.com). Makes a secondary market in student loans and helps students consolidate their existing loans. Programs include the SMART LOAN, Great Rewards, and Smart Rewards, which allow borrowers who repay their loans on time to get a reduction in the interest rate on the remaining balance of their loans.

U.S. Government

▶ IRS Publications. For free copies of these and other publications, visit your local IRS office, or call 800-829-3676, or see its Web site: http://www.irs.gov.

▶ IRS Publications 17 and 970. Information about federal income tax benefits associated with saving for college; for your free copy, visit your local IRS office, call the agency toll-free at 800-829-3676, or visit its Web site: http://www.irs.gov.

▶ IRS Publications 550 and 970. Information on the tax aspects of using savings bonds to pay for college.

▶ U.S. Department of Education, Federal Student Aid Program (400 Maryland Ave., S.W., Washington, DC 20202. Telephone: 800-433-3243; http://www.ed.gov). Oversees all federal student aid programs. Brochures include "Looking for Student Aid," "Funding Your Education," and "The Student Guide: Financial Aid from the U.S. Department of Education," which explains Pell grants, SEOGs, college work-study programs, Perkins loans, Stafford loans, and PLUS and SLS loans. Also publishes a useful guide titled *Preparing Your Child for College: A Resource Book for Parents.*

▶ U.S. Department of the Treasury; U.S. Savings Bonds. To check the current rates, call 800-487-2663. For more about the EasySaver plan, call 877-811-7283. For more about the education feature of U.S. Savings Bonds, see http://www.savingsbonds.gov or http://www.publicdebt.treas.gov or write to the Bureau of Public Debt, PO Box 1328, Parkersburg, WV 26106-1328. Telephone: 877-811-7283.

Military Sources of Financial Aid

▶ Air Force ROTC. HQ/RROO, 551 E. Maxwell Blvd., Maxwell Air Force Base, AL 36112-6106. Telephone: 205-953-2091; 800-522-0033, ext. 2091; http://www.afoats.af.mil), or see a local recruiter.

▶ Army ROTC. GoldQUEST Center, P.O. Box 3279, Warminster, PA 18974-0128. National headquarters at Fort Monroe, VA 23651-5238. Telephone: 800-USA-ROTC (http://www.tradoc.army.mil/index.html), or see a local recruiter.

▶ Navy and Marine Corps ROTC. 250 Dallas St., Naval Air Station, Pensacola, FL 32508-5220. Telephone: 904-452-4960; 800-NAV-ROTC (http://www.nrotc.navy.mil/aboutnrotc.cfm), or see a local recruiter.

Web Sites

▶ FAFSA, Department of Education, Office of Postsecondary Education (Telephone: 800-433-3243, 319-337-5665 http://www.fafsa.ed.gov). File your Free Application for Federal Student Aid (FAFSA) online (site offers detailed instructions on filling out the form and is loaded with links to colleges and other financial aid-related Web sites). If you have questions about filling out these forms, you can call the FAFSA Service Center at 800-801-0576.

▶ *FastWeb.com.* Find colleges and scholarships and apply online for the scholarship that suits your needs. The site has a lot of information on scholarships, loans, and grants and how to apply for them. Requires membership before making scholarship application. http://www.fastweb.com.

▶ *Fidelity.* In the College Planning section you will find a concise explanation of Section 529 college savings plans, along with comparisons of those plans with Custodian, Brokerage, Education IRA, and prepaid tuition plans. http://personal100.fidelity.com/planning/college/parents/chart-parents.html

▶ *FinAid!* A public service site, sponsored by the National Association of Student Financial Aid Administrators (NASFAA), allows you to ask questions of financial aid counselors; also provides information about college loans, scholarships, and grants. Assists you with financial aid applications, demystifies the paperwork, and provides forms and instructions. Includes 18 calculators and offers advice on college admissions and jobs. http://www.finaid.org

► *Saving for College.com.* This site provides a lot of information about Section 529 college savings plans. Includes details of all the state government college financing plans. Just select your state and the information comes up. http://www.savingforcollege.com

► *TIAA-CREF.* Serves as investment manager for state-sponsored college savings programs, education IRAs, prepaid tuition plans, and other college loans; charges an annual fee of .8 percent of account assets for its services. http://www.tiaa-cref.org/tuition/colgstat.html

► *TurboTax.* Learn about available education funding plans and the general tax implications for each; http://www.turbotax.com/index.php?redirect=yes&source=215cc1

► The *U.S. News and World Report*'s annual college edition provides a list of what the magazine evaluates as the best college values. Another part of the site guides you through the financial aid process. It answers frequently asked questions about financing college. The site also lists other financial aid Web sites, a loan center, and much more. http://www.usnews.com/usnews/edu/dollars/dshome.htm

Index